Table of Contents

Introduction 2-3
Week One 4-5
Week Two 6-7
Week Three 8-9
Week Four 10-11
Week Five 12-13
Week Six 14-15
Week Seven 16-17
Week Eight 18-19
Week Nine 20-21
Week Ten 22-23
Week Eleven 24-25
Week Twelve 26-27
Week Thirteen 28-29
Week Fourteen 30-31
Week Fifteen 32-33
Week Sixteen 34-35
Week Seventeen 36-37
Week Eighteen 38-39
Week Nineteen 40-41
Week Twenty 42-43
Week Twenty-One 44-45
Week Twenty-Two 46-47
Week Twenty-Three 48-49
Week Twenty-Four 50-51
Week Twenty-Five 52-53
Week Twenty-Six 54-55
Week Twenty-Seven 56-57
Week Twenty-Eight 58-59

Week Twenty-Nine 60-61
Week Thirty 62-63
Week Thirty-One 64-65
Week Thirty-Two 66-67
Week Thirty-Three 68-69
Week Thirty-Four 70-71
Week Thirty-Five 72-73
Week Thirty-Six 74-75
Assessment One 76
Assessment Two 77
Assessment Three 78
Assessment Four 79
Assessment Five 80
Assessment Six 81
Assessment Seven 82
Assessment Eight 83
Assessment Nine 84
Assessment Ten 85
Assessment Eleven 86
Assessment Twelve 87
Assessment Thirteen 88
Assessment Fourteen 89
Assessment Fifteen 90
Assessment Sixteen 91
Assessment Seventeen 92
Assessment Eighteen 93
Assessment Answer Key 94-96
Proofreader's Marks .... inside cover

Introduction to *Daily Oral Language Grade 2*

The purpose of the *Daily Oral Language* series is to provide teachers with an effective structure for teaching, reinforcing, and assessing students' oral and written language skills, proofreading skills, and test-taking proficiency. This is accomplished by combining brief, daily, oral exercises with regular multiple choice assessment tests. This combination of practice and reinforcement prepares students to write and edit their own work, and allows them to become proficient with common standardized test-taking procedures.

How This Book is Organized

This book is divided into daily oral exercises and biweekly standardized test assessments.
1. Daily Exercises (pages 4-75)
   - On each left hand page, you will find five daily lessons: two sentences to be corrected for each day of a thirty-six week school year.
   - On each right hand page, you will find an exercise answer key with corrections noted in red.
   - The answer key also includes a summary of skills addressed in each exercise, abbreviated as follows: C = capitalization, G = grammar, P = punctuation, and S = spelling.
2. Biweekly Assessments (pages 76-93)
   - Eighteen multiple choice assessment tests are included, presented in a standardized test format.
   - An answer key for the assessments is provided at the end of the section.

How to Use This Book

The exercises in this book should require about ten minutes of class time each day, and will be most effective if used as part of a regular class routine.
1. Make a transparency from each of the left-hand pages of the daily exercise section.
2. Present the incorrect sentences to students on an overhead projector, covering all but that day's sentences.
3. Call on students to orally identify and then correct the errors in each sentence. If desired, allow volunteers to use an overhead pen to mark the corrections on the transparency, and write the sentences correctly on the lines provided. Students may use the proofreader's marks on the inside back cover to aid them in this process.
4. At the end of each two-week period, have students complete the appropriate standardized test assessment.

Other Options for Presentation

Rather than presenting the Daily Oral Language exercises using an overhead projector, you may wish to:
- Photocopy and hand out Daily Oral Language exercise pages daily or weekly. Have students complete the exercises individually or as a group activity.

- Write incorrect sentences on a chalkboard or dry-erase board. Have student volunteers point out errors and make corrections on the board. Students can record corrected sentences in a Daily Oral Language notebook.

Daily Oral Language Extension Activities

The following is a list of quick follow-up activities that allow students to practice other language skills using the corrected Daily Oral Language sentences. Students can:

- Rewrite the sentences in a different tense.
- Identify the part of speech of each word in the sentences.
- Replace nouns with pronouns or proper nouns, and vice-versa.
- Rewrite the sentences as questions, statements, exclamations, etc.
- Identify the subject and predicate of each sentence.
- Write additional sentences, telling what might happen next.
- Rewrite the sentences by rearranging phrases and clauses.
- Use the proofreader's marks on the inside back cover to practice editing skills.

About the Skills Addressed in This Series

- Regardless of how many times a skill correction is made in a sentence, the corresponding abbreviation (C, G, P, or S) will appear only once in the skills summary.

- Noun/pronoun case agreement errors, verb tense and conjugation errors, subject-verb agreement errors, and word order errors are grammatical skill corrections (G). Capitalization (C), punctuation (P), and spelling (S) errors are easy to classify.

- Because spoken grammatical errors are transcribed as phonetic writing errors, incorrect homophone choices and enunciation errors have been categorized as spelling (S), rather than grammar (G) errors. For example, *Dontcha* for *Don't you*, *are* for *our*, and *there* for *they're* are categorized "S" in the skills summary.

- A grammatical correction made by eliminating a double subject is categorized (G) but is not further noted in the answer key. For example, *Jim he likes to draw* would appear in the answer key as *Jim likes to draw.* (G)

- When addressing commas in a series of three or more, a comma before *and* is included. For example: He, she, and I will go.

- Where appropriate, the abbreviations A.M. and P.M. are used for denoting time.

Week One

Rewrite the sentences correctly.

Monday	1. we have a birthday party last wedsday. _____ 2. me and bill played ball together. _____
Tuesday	1. She miss the bus last friday _____ 2. joe he have a broken arm. _____
Wednesday	1. Is labor day a national holiday _____ 2. the first day of school is in august _____
Thursday	1. we has many new student this year. _____ 2. jim and ray be in my class. _____
Friday	1. i gots a new puppy. _____ 2. The puppys name is buster. _____

Week One Answer Key
Corrected Sentences

Day		Sentences	Skills
Monday	1.	We had a birthday party last Wednesday.	C, G, S
	2.	Bill and I played ball together.	C, G
Tuesday	1.	She missed the bus last Friday.	C, G, P
	2.	Joe has a broken arm.	C, G
Wednesday	1.	Is Labor Day a national holiday?	C, P
	2.	The first day of school is in August.	C, P
Thursday	1.	We have many new students this year.	C, G
	2.	Jim and Ray are in my class.	C, G
Friday	1.	I have a new puppy.	C, G
	2.	The puppy's name is Buster.	C, P

Week Two

Rewrite the sentences correctly.

Monday	1. that boy taked the chair. _____ 2. they is playing with a puzzle _____
Tuesday	1. last sunday, we had a visitor. _____ 2. The visitors name was jack. _____
Wednesday	1. our techer talk abot playground rules. _____ 2. john and sue were not listen. _____
Thursday	1. me and my friend work well together. _____ 2. we was very good at adding the numbers. _____
Friday	1. linda have a letter from her friend. _____ 2. Her grandmother be mrs bell. _____

Week Two Answer Key

Corrected Sentences   **Skills**

Monday	1. That boy took the chair.	C, G
	2. They are playing with a puzzle.	C, G, P
Tuesday	1. Last Sunday, we had a visitor.	C
	2. The visitor's name was Jack.	C, P
Wednesday	1. Our teacher talked about playground rules.	C, G, S
	2. John and Sue were not listening.	C, G
Thursday	1. My friend and I work well together.	C, G
	2. We were very good at adding the numbers.	C, G
Friday	1. Linda has a letter from her friend.	C, G
	2. Her grandmother is Mrs. Bell.	C, G, P

Week Three

Name _____

Rewrite the sentences correctly.

Monday	1. Bill, jack, and david have fun together. _____ 2. They has been working on a drawing _____
Tuesday	1. Is that you hat on the chair _____ 2. I thought you leaved it here on friday. _____
Wednesday	1. My birthday were in october. _____ 2. we haved a birthday party yesterday. _____
Thursday	1. Mom are haveing a garage sale. _____ 2. Doug said, i woke up early today. _____
Friday	1. we maked a sign for the peeler school bake sale. _____ 2. Are new teacher is mrs. mills. _____

Week Three Answer Key

Corrected Sentences   **Skills**

Monday	1. Bill, Jack, and David have fun together.	C
	2. They have been working on a drawing.	G, P
Tuesday	1. Is that your hat on the chair?	G, P
	2. I thought you left it here on Friday.	C, G
Wednesday	1. My birthday was in October.	C, G
	2. We had a birthday party yesterday.	C, G
Thursday	1. Mom is having a garage sale.	G, S
	2. Doug said, "I woke up early today."	C, P
Friday	1. We made a sign for the Peeler School Bake Sale.	C, G
	2. Our new teacher is Mrs. Mills.	C, S

Week Four

Rewrite the sentences correctly.

Monday	1. dad taked a trip on sondey. _____ 2. jason said, There are a lot of people here. _____
Tuesday	1. My sister was borned august 5 1995. _____ 2. Her name be jane _____
Wednesday	1. Thrusday we will have a party for mary. _____ 2. me and jack be going to jacksonville. _____
Thursday	1. We dont want no candy. _____ 2. mrs johnson live next door to us. _____
Friday	1. gene wasnt at school yesterday. _____ 2. does we have time to play another game _____

Week Four Answer Key

		Skills
Monday	1. Dad took a trip on Sunday.	C, G, S
	2. Jason said, "There are a lot of people here."	C, P
Tuesday	1. My sister was born August 5, 1995.	C, G, P
	2. Her name is Jane.	C, G, P
Wednesday	1. Thursday we will have a party for Mary.	C, S
	2. Jack and I are going to Jacksonville.	C, G
Thursday	1. We don't want any candy.	G, P
	2. Mrs. Johnson lives next door to us.	C, G, P
Friday	1. Gene wasn't at school yesterday.	C, P
	2. Do we have time to play another game?	C, G, P

Week Five

Name _____

Rewrite the sentences correctly.

Monday

1. it have been a beautiful fall season

_____

2. me haft to take out the trash.

_____

Tuesday

1. We moved to ohio on june 10, 2000

_____

2. Have you ever been to denver colorado?

_____

Wednesday

1. They dont want to play no games.

_____

2. dad said, Very nice work!

_____

Thursday

1. Janie mow the grass last saturday.

_____

2. Did mrs lake say it would rain today

_____

Friday

1. i getted the package on Wendsdy.

_____

2. Dont they own two dog, too

_____

Week Five Answer Key

Corrected Sentences

		Skills
Monday	1. It has been a beautiful fall season.	C, G, P
	2. I have to take out the trash.	C, G, S
Tuesday	1. We moved to Ohio on June 10, 2000.	C, P
	2. Have you ever been to Denver, Colorado?	C, P
Wednesday	1. They don't want to play any games.	G, P
	2. Dad said, "Very nice work!"	C, P
Thursday	1. Janie mowed the grass last Saturday.	C, G
	2. Did Mrs. Lake say it would rain today?	C, P
Friday	1. I got the package on Wednesday.	C, G, S
	2. Don't they own two dogs, too?	G, P

Week Six

Rewrite the sentences correctly.

Monday

1. What time is dr benson come?

_____

2. is ms susan ball here yet?

_____

Tuesday

1. Joe ask, Is this the last page of the report?

_____

2. She lives on woodland drive in detroit.

_____

Wednesday

1. can we finesh the job by nex weekend

_____

2. Next monday be labor day.

_____

Thursday

1. we be takeing a long trip!

_____

2. we is going to lake james

_____

Friday

1. Tom axed, May I come with you?

_____

2. I want to go to mounds park in anderson.

_____

Week Six Answer Key
Corrected Sentences

Skills

		Skills
Monday	1. What time is Dr. Benson coming?	C, G, P
	2. Is Ms. Susan Ball here yet?	C, P
Tuesday	1. Joe asked, "Is this the last page of the report?"	G, P
	2. She lives on Woodland Drive in Detroit.	C
Wednesday	1. Can we finish the job by next weekend?	C, P, S
	2. Next Monday is Labor Day.	C, G
Thursday	1. We are taking a long trip!	C, G, S
	2. We are going to Lake James.	C, G, P
Friday	1. Tom asked, "May I come with you?"	P, S
	2. I want to go to Mounds Park in Anderson.	C

Week Seven

Rewrite the sentences correctly.

Monday	1. The sunnyhills cafe will open on sunday _____ 2. the store it will open at 8:00 in the morning _____
Tuesday	1. Soccer practice begin next monday. _____ 2. jill and me am going camping tomorrow. _____
Wednesday	1. He lives in st louis missouri. _____ 2. Her move here last december. _____
Thursday	1. there be five peeple in my family. _____ 2. Their address is 401 north hayden street. _____
Friday	1. do mike attend maplecrest middle school? _____ 2. Carlas techer is mrs steuben. _____

Week Seven Answer Key

Corrected Sentences

		Skills
Monday	1. The Sunnyhills Cafe will open on Sunday.	C, P
	2. The store will open at 8:00 in the morning.	C, G, P
Tuesday	1. Soccer practice begins next Monday.	C, G
	2. Jill and I are going camping tomorrow.	C, G
Wednesday	1. He lives in St. Louis, Missouri.	C, P
	2. She moved here last December.	C, G
Thursday	1. There are five people in my family.	C, G, S
	2. Their address is 401 North Hayden Street.	C
Friday	1. Does Mike attend Maplecrest Middle School?	C, G
	2. Carla's teacher is Mrs. Steuben.	C, P, S

Week Eight

Rewrite the sentences correctly.

Monday	1. we has play practice all next week. _____ 2. The play be called great presidents. _____
Tuesday	1. Mrs. casta is plan our fall festival. _____ 2. jills mother, mrs blake, is baking cookies. _____
Wednesday	1. will the class party be on october 30 _____ 2. Phil asked, May I bring treets, too? _____
Thursday	1. The students is excite abot the party. _____ 2. Bill he is going to leed the games. _____
Friday	1. My favrite game is duck, duck, goose. _____ 2. Isnt kims cat named tiger? _____

Week Eight Answer Key
Corrected Sentences

		Skills
Monday	1. We have play practice all next week.	C, G
	2. The play is called Great Presidents.	C, G
Tuesday	1. Mrs. Casta is planning our Fall Festival.	C, G
	2. Jill's mother, Mrs. Blake, is baking cookies.	C, P
Wednesday	1. Will the class party be on October 30?	C, P
	2. Phil asked, "May I bring treats, too?"	P, S
Thursday	1. The students are excited about the party.	G, S
	2. Bill is going to lead the games.	G, S
Friday	1. My favorite game is Duck, Duck, Goose.	C, S
	2. Isn't Kim's cat named Tiger?	C, P

Week Nine

Name _____

Rewrite the sentences correctly.

Monday	1. We cudnt go on the feeld trip. _____ 2. carol were very sleepy. _____
Tuesday	1. We took a trip on november 22 1999. _____ 2. we seen them on a wednesday nite. _____
Wednesday	1. Our class visited gregs pumpkin farm. _____ 2. Its on eighth street in farmville. _____
Thursday	1. Jim said, I cant go that day. _____ 2. Why aint you going to the game _____
Friday	1. Me and jenny we enjoyed the trip! _____ 2. Lets rite a letter to mr. johnson. _____

Week Nine Answer Key
Corrected Sentences

		Skills
Monday	1. We couldn't go on the field trip.	P, S
	2. Carol was very sleepy.	C, G
Tuesday	1. We took a trip on November 22, 1999.	C, P
	2. We saw them on a Wednesday night.	C, G, S
Wednesday	1. Our class visited Greg's Pumpkin Farm.	C, P
	2. It's on Eighth Street in Farmville.	C, P
Thursday	1. Jim said, "I can't go that day."	P
	2. Why aren't you going to the game?	G, P
Friday	1. Jenny and I enjoyed the trip!	C, G
	2. Let's write a letter to Mr. Johnson.	C, P, S

Week Ten

Name _____

Rewrite the sentences correctly.

Monday	1. me and sid we need a ride to school. _____ 2. Ken said, What time is it now? _____
Tuesday	1. What is you wearing to the halloween party _____ 2. The party will be called a haunted classroom. _____
Wednesday	1. We will begin friday at 100 in the afternoon. _____ 2. jills mother are in the other room. _____
Thursday	1. halloween are on october 31. _____ 2. Phil sayed, Will Friday ever come _____
Friday	1. mollys costume be a bumblebee. _____ 2. Bob said, My father is comeing to help. _____

Week Ten Answer Key

Corrected Sentences

		Skills
Monday	1. Sid and I need a ride to school.	C, G
	2. Ken said, "What time is it now?"	P
Tuesday	1. What are you wearing to the Halloween party?	C, G, P
	2. The party will be called A Haunted Classroom.	C
Wednesday	1. We will begin Friday at 1:00 in the afternoon.	C, P
	2. Jill's mother is in the other room.	C, G, P
Thursday	1. Halloween is on October 31.	C, G
	2. Phil said, "Will Friday ever come?"	P, S
Friday	1. Molly's costume is a bumblebee.	C, G, P
	2. Bob said, "My father is coming to help."	P, S

Week Eleven

Rewrite the sentences correctly.

Monday	1. november 19, 2000 were a snowy day. _____ 2. lee and donna weared there winter coats. _____
Tuesday	1. Janes mom, mrs. jolly, bought her a new coat. _____ 2. My house it be on Delaware street. _____
Wednesday	1. A man come to fiks the furnace on Tuesday. _____ 2. We dint have heat for over too hours _____
Thursday	1. It should have been fix yestday. _____ 2. Our team is the east central tigers. _____
Friday	1. We was happy win the heet came on. _____ 2. mike and me taked off our hats. _____

Week Eleven Answer Key

Corrected Sentences

Skills

		Skills
Monday	1. November 19, 2000 was a snowy day.	C, G
	2. Lee and Donna wore their winter coats.	C, G, S
Tuesday	1. Jane's mom, Mrs. Jolly, bought her a new coat.	C, P
	2. My house is on Delaware Street.	C, G
Wednesday	1. A man came to fix the furnace on Tuesday.	G, S
	2. We didn't have heat for over two hours.	P, S
Thursday	1. It should have been fixed yesterday.	G, S
	2. Our team is the East Central Tigers.	C
Friday	1. We were happy when the heat came on.	G, S
	2. Mike and I took off our hats.	C, G

Week Twelve

Rewrite the sentences correctly.

Monday

1. I was invited to jimmy browns house.

_____

2. My best frend be carl lentz.

_____

Tuesday

1. jimmy and me are going skateing.

_____

2. jimmys mom are a great cook!

_____

Wednesday

1. The browns live at 606 west poplar lane.

_____

2. We had a grete time lass night

_____

Thursday

1. I falled down and bump my head.

_____

2. didnt we skate until 830

_____

Friday

1. jimmy said, i cant wait to go again!

_____

2. Lets join the skyville skate club!

_____

Week Twelve Answer Key

Corrected Sentences

		Skills
Monday	1. I was invited to Jimmy Brown's house.	C, P
	2. My best friend is Carl Lentz.	C, G, S
Tuesday	1. Jimmy and I are going skating.	C, G, S
	2. Jimmy's mom is a great cook!	C, G, P
Wednesday	1. The Browns live at 606 West Poplar Lane.	C
	2. We had a great time last night.	P, S
Thursday	1. I fell down and bumped my head.	G
	2. Didn't we skate until 8:30?	C, P
Friday	1. Jimmy said, "I can't wait to go again!"	C, P
	2. Let's join the Skyville Skate Club!	C, P

Week Thirteen

Rewrite the sentences correctly.

Monday	1. Mr. and mrs smeltzer lives down the street. _____ 2. There daughter she is in my class. _____
Tuesday	1. We is haveing a special program next week. _____ 2. it has rain for two days now. _____
Wednesday	1. Well has to play our game another dey. _____ 2. i hop the rain will stop soon. _____
Thursday	1. when was you borned _____ 2. Him was born october 2 1970. _____
Friday	1. uncle steve and aunt aretha came to visit me. _____ 2. i is the oldest of six childrens. _____

Week Thirteen Answer Key

Corrected Sentences

Monday	1. Mr. and Mrs. Smeltzer live down the street.	C, G, P
	2. Their daughter is in my class.	G, S
Tuesday	1. We are having a special program next week.	G, S
	2. It has rained for two days now.	C, G
Wednesday	1. We'll have to play our game another day.	G, P, S
	2. I hope the rain will stop soon.	C, S
Thursday	1. When were you born?	C, G, P
	2. He was born October 2, 1970.	C, G, P
Friday	1. Uncle Steve and Aunt Aretha came to visit me.	C
	2. I am the oldest of six children.	C, G

© Carson-Dellosa CD-0042   C = Capitalization, G = Grammar, P = Punctuation, S = Spelling   29

Week Fourteen

Rewrite the sentences correctly.

Monday

1. Is their a holiday this weak?

   _____

2. Lets eat dinner at grandma tillys house!

   _____

Tuesday

1. Are we in school may 15 2007

   _____

2. Can you gess wat holiday today is?

   _____

Wednesday

1. I hope meny people will came to our house.

   _____

2. My cousin angela she cant come.

   _____

Thursday

1. We will celebrate on Fridey evenin.

   _____

2. My grandma she always cook the bestest food.

   _____

Friday

1. isnt thanksgiving on a thursday

   _____

2. Ill be there at 900 in the morning.

30

Week Fourteen Answer Key

Corrected Sentences

Day	Sentences	Skills
Monday	1. Is there a holiday this week?	S
	2. Let's eat dinner at Grandma Tilly's house!	C, P
Tuesday	1. Are we in school May 15, 2007?	C, P
	2. Can you guess what holiday today is?	S
Wednesday	1. I hope many people will come to our house.	G, S
	2. My cousin Angela can't come.	C, G, P
Thursday	1. We will celebrate on Friday evening.	S
	2. My grandma always cooks the best food.	G
Friday	1. Isn't Thanksgiving on a Thursday?	C, P
	2. I'll be there at 9:00 in the morning.	P

© Carson-Dellosa CD-0042   C = Capitalization, G = Grammar, P = Punctuation, S = Spelling   31

Week Fifteen

Name _____

Rewrite the sentences correctly.

Monday	1. we is going shopping after skool today. _____ 2. steve, don, and beth is coming, too. _____
Tuesday	1. on december 15 2003, we will have a party. _____ 2. me and aaron is decorating the room. _____
Wednesday	1. The show will be tuesday at 300. _____ 2. wont the chorus sing this year _____
Thursday	1. miss thorsons class is werking on a play. _____ 2. We are riting invitations to or parents. _____
Friday	1. Lunch will be serve erly on december 15. _____ 2. Sues mom said, Would you likes a healthy snack? _____

Week Fifteen Answer Key

Corrected Sentences

Day	Sentences	Skills
Monday	1. We are going shopping after school today.	C, G, S
	2. Steve, Don, and Beth are coming, too.	C, G
Tuesday	1. On December 15, 2003, we will have a party.	C, P
	2. Aaron and I are decorating the room.	C, G
Wednesday	1. The show will be Tuesday at 3:00.	C, P
	2. Won't the chorus sing this year?	C, P
Thursday	1. Miss Thorson's class is working on a play.	C, P, S
	2. We are writing invitations to our parents.	S
Friday	1. Lunch will be served early on December 15.	C, G, S
	2. Sue's mom said, "Would you like a healthy snack?"	G, P

Week Sixteen

Rewrite the sentences correctly.

Monday	1. Jackie said, Well be here until 245. _____ 2. Jay said, i think everything is great! _____
Tuesday	1. Our partay will be befor christmas. _____ 2. it be the same day as our winter braik. _____
Wednesday	1. We dont have no cookies for the party. _____ 2. lisa have a pensul and two notebook. _____
Thursday	1. I rote a story called the quiet hero. _____ 2. me need to shrapen my pencil. _____
Friday	1. i finded sum paper on the floor. _____ 2. miss handley show us her new computer. _____

Week Sixteen Answer Key

Corrected Sentences

		Skills
Monday	1. Jackie said, "We'll be here until 2:45."	P
	2. Jay said, "I think everything is great!"	C, P
Tuesday	1. Our party will be before Christmas.	C, S
	2. It is the same day as our winter break.	C, G, S
Wednesday	1. We don't have any cookies for the party.	G, P
	2. Lisa has a pencil and two notebooks.	C, G, S
Thursday	1. I wrote a story called <u>The Quiet Hero</u>.	C, S
	2. I need to sharpen my pencil.	C, G, S
Friday	1. I found some paper on the floor.	C, G, S
	2. Miss Handley showed us her new computer.	C, G

Week Seventeen

Rewrite the sentences correctly.

Monday	1. greta she seen snowflakes falling.
	_____
	2. jerry asked, Is it still snowing?
	_____
Tuesday	1. The snow falled to times last nite.
	_____
	2. we shovel snow for for hours.
	_____
Wednesday	1. We stayd home on new years day.
	_____
	2. mom she made turkey, peas, and a big cake
	_____
Thursday	1. My cousin erin she comed to visit.
	_____
	2. We eat alot of food at dinner last night.
	_____
Friday	1. That holiday was january 1 2000.
	_____
	2. wasnt that a special day
	_____

Week Seventeen Answer Key

Corrected Sentences   **Skills**

	Corrected Sentences	Skills
Monday	1. Greta saw snowflakes falling.	C, G
	2. Jerry asked, "Is it still snowing?"	C, P
Tuesday	1. The snow fell two times last night.	G, S
	2. We shoveled snow for four hours.	C, G, S
Wednesday	1. We stayed home on New Year's Day.	C, P, S
	2. Mom made turkey, peas, and a big cake.	C, G, P
Thursday	1. My cousin Erin came to visit.	C, G
	2. We ate a lot of food at dinner last night.	G, S
Friday	1. That holiday was January 1, 2000.	C, P
	2. Wasn't that a special day?	C, P

Week Eighteen

Rewrite the sentences correctly.

Monday	1. On tuesday, well watch a film about animuls. _____ 2. Anna said, Its the best film ever! _____
Tuesday	1. there was only too students absent yesterday. _____ 2. sarah and janet was not their. _____
Wednesday	1. mr watts he showed us a log cabin. _____ 2. It was a model of abraham lincolns cabin. _____
Thursday	1. We saw the model on january 7 2001. _____ 2. her said, I relly learned a lot. _____
Friday	1. Ill meet you rite after school. _____ 2. i didnt no that the cabin were so small. _____

Week Eighteen Answer Key

Corrected Sentences

		Skills
Monday	1. On Tuesday, we'll watch a film about animals.	C, P, S
	2. Anna said, "It's the best film ever!"	P
Tuesday	1. There were only two students absent yesterday.	C, G, S
	2. Sarah and Janet were not there.	C, G, S
Wednesday	1. Mr. Watts showed us a log cabin.	C, G, P
	2. It was a model of Abraham Lincoln's cabin.	C, P
Thursday	1. We saw the model on January 7, 2001.	C, P
	2. She said, "I really learned a lot."	C, G, P, S
Friday	1. I'll meet you right after school.	P, S
	2. I didn't know that the cabin was so small.	C, G, P, S

© Carson-Dellosa CD-0042   C = Capitalization, G = Grammar, P = Punctuation, S = Spelling   39

Week Nineteen

Rewrite the sentences correctly.

Monday	1. Lets make a display for the hole school to see. _____ 2. Is your address 706 east wilson avenue _____
Tuesday	1. Our game will be play at 245 today. _____ 2. it will be at grover elementary school. _____
Wednesday	1. Well play against the hamilton bulldogs. _____ 2. they is a tough team to beat. _____
Thursday	1. ron said, I hope we win both games. _____ 2. The gym are located at 611 west school road. _____
Friday	1. mom and dad they are comeing to the game. _____ 2. alysa will mete you at 230 on saturday. _____

Week Nineteen Answer Key

Corrected Sentences

Skills

Monday	1. Let's make a display for the whole school to see.	P, S
	2. Is your address 706 East Wilson Avenue?	C, P
Tuesday	1. Our game will be played at 2:45 today.	G, P
	2. It will be at Grover Elementary School.	C
Wednesday	1. We'll play against the Hamilton Bulldogs.	C, P
	2. They are a tough team to beat.	C, G
Thursday	1. Ron said, "I hope we win both games."	C, P
	2. The gym is located at 611 West School Road.	C, G
Friday	1. Mom and Dad are coming to the game.	C, G, S
	2. Alysa will meet you at 2:30 on Saturday.	C, P, S

Week Twenty

Rewrite the sentences correctly.

Monday	1. i has to wash the dishes and sweep the flor. _____ 2. theyll be here around 600 today. _____
Tuesday	1. we was play in the snow. _____ 2. Mom said, its time to come in now. _____
Wednesday	1. It was snow on january 13 2001. _____ 2. That were a day well never forget! _____
Thursday	1. mike and me made snow castles. _____ 2. vince said, id like to help! _____
Friday	1. george washington he is tims favorite president. _____ 2. Sherrys favorite leader is president lincoln. _____

Week Twenty Answer Key

Corrected Sentences   Skills

Monday	1. I have to wash the dishes and sweep the floor.	C, G, S
	2. They'll be here around 6:00 today.	C, P
Tuesday	1. We were playing in the snow.	C, G
	2. Mom said, "It's time to come in now."	C, P
Wednesday	1. It was snowing on January 13, 2001.	C, G, P
	2. That was a day we'll never forget!	G, P
Thursday	1. Mike and I made snow castles.	C, G
	2. Vince said, "I'd like to help!"	C, P
Friday	1. George Washington is Tim's favorite president.	C, G, P
	2. Sherry's favorite leader is President Lincoln.	C, P

Week Twenty-One

Rewrite the sentences correctly.

Monday	1. Im going to the dentist on february 4 2003. _____ 2. joyces sister is fore feet tall. _____
Tuesday	1. Theyre mom picked us up erly. _____ 2. It were snowing heavily by 330. _____
Wednesday	1. me and vincent goed outside to play. _____ 2. i taked home a gud book to read. _____
Thursday	1. are you reddy to go sledding _____ 2. she said, Of course i am! _____
Friday	1. we come home very tired today. _____ 2. i ate, tuk a bath, and goed to bed. _____

Week Twenty-One Answer Key

Corrected Sentences

		Skills
Monday	1. I'm going to the dentist on February 4, 2003.	C, P
	2. Joyce's sister is four feet tall.	C, P, S
Tuesday	1. Their mom picked us up early.	S
	2. It was snowing heavily by 3:30.	G, P
Wednesday	1. Vincent and I went outside to play.	C, G
	2. I took home a good book to read.	C, G, S
Thursday	1. Are you ready to go sledding?	C, P, S
	2. She said, "Of course I am!"	C, P
Friday	1. We came home very tired today.	C, G
	2. I ate, took a bath, and went to bed.	C, G, S

Week Twenty-Two

Name _____

Rewrite the sentences correctly.

Monday	1. Well have a party february 14 2002. _____ 2. Hank said, This holiday is my favrite! _____
Tuesday	1. Are class will celebrate valentines day. _____ 2. Shea axed, Can we make cards today? _____
Wednesday	1. mr and mrs hill will bring the snacks. _____ 2. They is Steves parents. _____
Thursday	1. The party it will be holded on friday. _____ 2. i gived cards to everyone in mi class. _____
Friday	1. becky asked, What games will we play _____ 2. me and my frends will have a lot of fun. _____

Week Twenty-Two Answer Key

Corrected Sentences

Skills

		Skills
Monday	1. We'll have a party February 14, 2002.	C, P
	2. Hank said, "This holiday is my favorite!"	P, S
Tuesday	1. Our class will celebrate Valentine's Day.	C, P, S
	2. Shea asked, "Can we make cards today?"	P, S
Wednesday	1. Mr. and Mrs. Hill will bring the snacks.	C, P
	2. They are Steve's parents.	G, P
Thursday	1. The party will be held on Friday.	C, G
	2. I gave cards to everyone in my class.	C, G, S
Friday	1. Becky asked, "What games will we play?"	C, P
	2. My friends and I will have a lot of fun.	C, G, S

Week Twenty-Three

Rewrite the sentences correctly.

Monday	1. my sister she breaked a dish this morning. _____ 2. Mom asked, How did it happen _____
Tuesday	1. She said, It slip out of my hand. _____ 2. Tim said, "It were an accident, mom." _____
Wednesday	1. We had a substitute teacher on wednsday. _____ 2. My sester and me had homework that nite. _____
Thursday	1. mr potts comed back on Tewsday. _____ 2. He said, "im hapy to be back." _____
Friday	1. We mist him on february 23 2000 _____ 2. i forgetted to bring the story that i wrote. _____

Week Twenty-Three Answer Key

Corrected Sentences

		Skills
Monday	1. My sister broke a dish this morning.	C, G
	2. Mom asked, "How did it happen?"	P
Tuesday	1. She said, "It slipped out of my hand."	G, P
	2. Tim said, "It was an accident, Mom."	C, G
Wednesday	1. We had a substitute teacher on Wednesday.	C, S
	2. My sister and I had homework that night.	C, G, S
Thursday	1. Mr. Potts came back on Tuesday.	C, G, P, S
	2. He said, "I'm happy to be back."	C, P, S
Friday	1. We missed him on February 23, 2000.	C, P, S
	2. I forgot to bring the story that I wrote.	C, G

Week Twenty-Four

Name _____

Rewrite the sentences correctly.

Monday

1. The bell ringed erly today

_____

2. She choosed a nise pair of gloves

_____

Tuesday

1. march 5 2000 was the date of the fire drill.

_____

2. i think it were a thrusday.

_____

Wednesday

1. the fire drill scared ray and I.

_____

2. it were a vary loud bell.

_____

Thursday

1. i almost scream!

_____

2. other people they was afraid, too.

_____

Friday

1. mrs tuttle she calm us down.

_____

2. we realy likes her alot.

_____

Week Twenty-Four Answer Key

Corrected Sentences   **Skills**

Monday	1. The bell rang early today.	G, P, S
	2. She chose a nice pair of gloves.	G, P, S
Tuesday	1. March 5, 2000 was the date of the fire drill.	C, P
	2. I think it was a Thursday.	C, G, S
Wednesday	1. The fire drill scared Ray and me.	C, G
	2. It was a very loud bell.	C, G, S
Thursday	1. I almost screamed!	C, G
	2. Other people were afraid, too.	C, G
Friday	1. Mrs. Tuttle calmed us down.	C, G, P
	2. We really like her a lot.	C, G, S

Week Twenty-Five

Name _____

Rewrite the sentences correctly.

Monday	1. on wednesday, we created our own books _____ 2. i drawed a picher on every page. _____
Tuesday	1. we took are books home. _____ 2. Wear is my favorite shoes _____
Wednesday	1. Mrs Turner sayed, No running! _____ 2. we dont want to miss the bus. _____
Thursday	1. They have a dog name meyer. _____ 2. He be blak and brown _____
Friday	1. laura and cathy likes to play with him. _____ 2. him be a vary friendly puppy. _____

Week Twenty-Five Answer Key
Corrected Sentences

		Skills
Monday	1. On Wednesday, we created our own books.	C, P
	2. I drew a picture on every page.	C, G, S
Tuesday	1. We took our books home.	C, S
	2. Where are my favorite shoes?	G, P, S
Wednesday	1. Mrs. Turner said, "No running!"	P, S
	2. We don't want to miss the bus.	C, P
Thursday	1. They have a dog named Meyer.	C, G
	2. He is black and brown.	G, P, S
Friday	1. Laura and Cathy like to play with him.	C, G
	2. He is a very friendly puppy.	C, G, S

Week Twenty-Six

Rewrite the sentences correctly.

Monday	1. we will has a vacation next week
	_____
	2. liz said, Will we be out all week?
	_____

Tuesday	1. my brother and me cant wait to leave.
	_____
	2. this will be our furst break in a long time
	_____

Wednesday	1. no, we wont be staying home.
	_____
	2. The breke begin next Mondy.
	_____

Thursday	1. that day, were going to my cousins house.
	_____
	2. im relly excite about next week.
	_____

Friday	1. is you family going to north carolina
	_____
	2. well be staying at 4320 emerald drive.
	_____

Week Twenty-Six Answer Key
Corrected Sentences

Monday	1. We will have a vacation next week.	C, G, P
	2. Liz said, "Will we be out all week?"	C, P
Tuesday	1. My brother and I can't wait to leave.	C, G, P
	2. This will be our first break in a long time.	C, P, S
Wednesday	1. No, we won't be staying home.	C, P
	2. The break begins next Monday.	G, S
Thursday	1. That day, we're going to my cousin's house.	C, P
	2. I'm really excited about next week.	C, G, P, S
Friday	1. Is your family going to North Carolina?	C, G, P
	2. We'll be staying at 4320 Emerald Drive.	C, P

Week Twenty-Seven

Rewrite the sentences correctly.

Monday	1. there is only to days before spring break. _____ 2. grandpa jones want us to visit. _____
Tuesday	1. I goed there march 24 2000. _____ 2. Dad said, Isnt she a great cook? _____
Wednesday	1. grandma readed storys to us yesterday. _____ 2. she are mi favrit teacher. _____
Thursday	1. Helen she said, What does you want for dinner? _____ 2. My brother sayed, Lets have steak! _____
Friday	1. what day does you leave for the mountains _____ 2. Our dance classes be on teusdays. _____

Week Twenty-Seven Answer Key

Corrected Sentences

Day	Sentence	Skills
Monday	1. There are only two days before spring break.	C, G, S
	2. Grandpa Jones wants us to visit.	C, G
Tuesday	1. I went there March 24, 2000.	C, G, P
	2. Dad said, "Isn't she a great cook?"	P
Wednesday	1. Grandma read stories to us yesterday.	C, G, S
	2. She is my favorite teacher.	C, G, S
Thursday	1. Helen said, "What do you want for dinner?"	G, P
	2. My brother said, "Let's have steak!"	P, S
Friday	1. What day do you leave for the mountains?	C, G, P
	2. Our dance classes are on Tuesdays.	C, G, S

Week Twenty-Eight

Name _____

Rewrite the sentences correctly.

Monday

1. it be a very sunny day today.

_____

2. sue said, Maybe spring is almost here!

_____

Tuesday

1. It was 70 degree on april 5 2000.

_____

2. i weared my jacket outside

_____

Wednesday

1. do you think spring be just arond the corner?

_____

2. i seed a flock of birds today.

_____

Thursday

1. on thursday, it were 80 degrees.

_____

2. We didnt need no jackets that day!

_____

Friday

1. wheres my winter coat

_____

2. it is a beutufull day.

_____

Week Twenty-Eight Answer Key

Corrected Sentences

Skills

Monday	1. It is a very sunny day today.	C, G
	2. Sue said, "Maybe spring is almost here!"	C, P
Tuesday	1. It was 70 degrees on April 5, 2000.	C, G, P
	2. I wore my jacket outside.	C, G, P
Wednesday	1. Do you think spring is just around the corner?	C, G, S
	2. I saw a flock of birds today.	C, G
Thursday	1. On Thursday, it was 80 degrees.	C, G
	2. We didn't need any jackets that day!	G, P
Friday	1. Where's my winter coat?	C, P
	2. It is a beautiful day.	C, S

Week Twenty-Nine

Rewrite the sentences correctly.

Name _____

Monday

1. witch book does you want to read next

_____

2. Thats the book i likes best.

_____

Tuesday

1. me desk are very messy

_____

2. us didnt finish until 900 at night.

_____

Wednesday

1. i show erik my coin collection yesterday.

_____

2. wayne brung some stamps to school.

_____

Thursday

1. The frog jump of of the table.

_____

2. The frog it land under sues desk.

_____

Friday

1. The book sale was on april 11 2000.

_____

2. it were setted up on the playground.

_____

Week Twenty-Nine Answer Key

Corrected Sentences

		Skills
Monday	1. Which book do you want to read next?	C, G, P, S
	2. That's the book I like best.	C, G, P
Tuesday	1. My desk is very messy.	C, G, P
	2. We didn't finish until 9:00 at night.	C, G, P
Wednesday	1. I showed Erik my coin collection yesterday.	C, G
	2. Wayne brought some stamps to school.	C, G
Thursday	1. The frog jumped off of the table.	G, S
	2. The frog landed under Sue's desk.	C, G, P
Friday	1. The book sale was on April 11, 2000.	C, P
	2. It was set up on the playground.	C, G

Week Thirty

Name _____

Rewrite the sentences correctly.

Monday	1. We visit the parkland zoo on april 15 2000. _____ 2. is that near niagra falls _____
Tuesday	1. buck and andrew they was absent. _____ 2. they miss a relly great trip. _____
Wednesday	1. We said, Thank you, miss frazier! _____ 2. do you know dr anita job? _____
Thursday	1. johns temperature waz high that day. _____ 2. Have you ever visit the seaside aquarium _____
Friday	1. our feeld trip were on Wednasday. _____ 2. we leaved after the bell ringed _____

Week Thirty Answer Key
Corrected Sentences

Day			Skills
Monday	1.	We visited the Parkland Zoo on April 15, 2000.	C, G, P
	2.	Is that near Niagra Falls?	C, P
Tuesday	1.	Buck and Andrew were absent.	C, G
	2.	They missed a really great trip.	C, G, S
Wednesday	1.	We said, "Thank you, Miss Frazier!"	C, P
	2.	Do you know Dr. Anita Job?	C, P
Thursday	1.	John's temperature was high that day.	C, P, S
	2.	Have you ever visited the Seaside Aquarium?	C, G, P
Friday	1.	Our field trip was on Wednesday.	C, G, S
	2.	We left after the bell rang.	C, G, P

Week Thirty-One

Rewrite the sentences correctly.

Name _____

Monday

1. We haved a musik program last week

_____

2. The program were call springtime magic

_____

Tuesday

1. Sum songs was give to students to sing.

_____

2. The recital taked place on april 23 2000.

_____

Wednesday

1. Our techer said, you did a great job!

_____

2. mr and mrs perkins be helping with the music

_____

Thursday

1. waz their singing and dancing last night

_____

2. thursday are the day of the race.

_____

Friday

1. bobs parents couldnt be there.

_____

2. They said, were relly sorry!

_____

Week Thirty-One Answer Key
Corrected Sentences

		Skills
Monday	1. We had a music program last week.	G, P, S
	2. The program was called Springtime Magic.	C, G, P
Tuesday	1. Some songs were given to students to sing.	G, S
	2. The recital took place on April 23, 2000.	C, G, P
Wednesday	1. Our teacher said, "You did a great job!"	C, P, S
	2. Mr. and Mrs. Perkins are helping with the music.	C, G, P
Thursday	1. Was there singing and dancing last night?	C, P, S
	2. Thursday is the day of the race.	C, G
Friday	1. Bob's parents couldn't be there.	C, P
	2. They said, "We're really sorry!"	C, P, S

© Carson-Dellosa CD-0042   C = Capitalization, G = Grammar, P = Punctuation, S = Spelling   65

Week Thirty-Two

Rewrite the sentences correctly.

Monday

1. college park school are having a celebration.

_____

2. It will be takeing plase next thursday.

_____

Tuesday

1. On may 1 2000, we had a big celebration

_____

2. we weared ribbons in our hair

_____

Wednesday

1. Everyone gone outside on may day.

_____

2. My parents said, We likes them blue and green ribbons!

_____

Thursday

1. Our May Day celebration were on tuesday.

_____

2. it were in the afternoon.

_____

Friday

1. It was the bestest may day celebrayshun ever!

_____

2. our principal, mr shaffer, he enjoyed the show.

_____

Week Thirty-Two Answer Key

Corrected Sentences

Skills

Monday	1. College Park School is having a celebration.	C, G
	2. It will be taking place next Thursday.	C, S
Tuesday	1. On May 1, 2000, we had a big celebration.	C, P
	2. We wore ribbons in our hair.	C, G, P
Wednesday	1. Everyone went outside on May Day.	C, G
	2. My parents said, "We like those blue and green ribbons!"	G, P
Thursday	1. Our May Day celebration was on Tuesday.	C, G
	2. It was in the afternoon.	C, G
Friday	1. It was the best May Day celebration ever!	C, G, S
	2. Our principal, Mr. Shaffer, enjoyed the show.	C, G, P

Week Thirty-Three

Rewrite the sentences correctly.

Monday	1. What do you whant to where to school _____ 2. The sun come out after it stop raining _____
Tuesday	1. Jake he said, The test was vary hard _____ 2. i finish the test late. _____
Wednesday	1. The test were on may 8 2010. _____ 2. im going to see the doctor on mondey. _____
Thursday	1. our teacher toll us to study this weekend. _____ 2. Jack said i guess I didnt study enough. _____
Friday	1. The test were given on friday. _____ 2. we taked the test after lunch _____

Week Thirty-Three Answer Key

Corrected Sentences

		Skills
Monday	1. What do you want to wear to school?	P, S
	2. The sun came out after it stopped raining.	G, P
Tuesday	1. Jake said, "The test was very hard."	G, P, S
	2. I finished the test late.	C, G
Wednesday	1. The test was on May 8, 2010.	C, G, P
	2. I'm going to see the doctor on Monday.	C, P, S
Thursday	1. Our teacher told us to study this weekend.	C, S
	2. Jack said, "I guess I didn't study enough."	C, P
Friday	1. The test was given on Friday.	C, G
	2. We took the test after lunch.	C, G, P

Week Thirty-Four

Rewrite the sentences correctly.

Monday

1. i loves to rede books.

_____

2. on may 18 2007, our school held a field day.

_____

Tuesday

1. Our gym teacher, miss donley, organize the games.

_____

2. her and mr havens was working together

_____

Wednesday

1. many student talked about the fun they haved.

_____

2. me and john we liked the water balloon toss.

_____

Thursday

1. Our feeld day was on may 21 2002.

_____

2. it were during the afternoon.

_____

Friday

1. What book does you want to share

_____

2. Dan said I forgot to bring my favrite book.

_____

Week Thirty-Four Answer Key

Corrected Sentences

		Skills
Monday	1. I love to read books.	C, G, S
	2. On May 18, 2007, our school held a Field Day.	C, P
Tuesday	1. Our gym teacher, Miss Donley, organized the games.	C, G
	2. She and Mr. Havens were working together.	C, G, P
Wednesday	1. Many students talked about the fun they had.	C, G
	2. John and I liked the water balloon toss.	C, G
Thursday	1. Our Field Day was on May 21, 2002.	C, P, S
	2. It was during the afternoon.	C, G
Friday	1. What book do you want to share?	G, P
	2. Dan said, "I forgot to bring my favorite book."	P, S

Week Thirty-Five

Name _____

Rewrite the sentences correctly.

Monday	1. Well start our vacation on june 6 2006. _____ 2. Dad said We will go to nashville tennessee. _____
Tuesday	1. my family be goin to the mountains for a week. _____ 2. I cant wait to see the blue ridge mountains. _____
Wednesday	1. Well be staying with mr and mrs robert hood _____ 2. Bobs children attend blue ridge elementary school. _____
Thursday	1. We will leave nex saterday morning. _____ 2. its over 100 mile to nashville _____
Friday	1. dad want us to help pack the car. _____ 2. we haf to leev early in the morning. _____

Week Thirty-Five Answer Key

Corrected Sentences

		Skills
Monday	1. We'll start our vacation on June 6, 2006.	C, P
	2. Dad said, "We will go to Nashville, Tennessee."	C, P
Tuesday	1. My family is going to the mountains for a week.	C, G, S
	2. I can't wait to see the Blue Ridge Mountains.	C, P
Wednesday	1. We'll be staying with Mr. and Mrs. Robert Hood.	C, P
	2. Bob's children attend Blue Ridge Elementary School.	C, P
Thursday	1. We will leave next Saturday morning.	C, S
	2. It's over 100 miles to Nashville.	C, G, P
Friday	1. Dad wants us to help pack the car.	C, G
	2. We have to leave early in the morning.	C, S

Week Thirty-Six

Rewrite the sentences correctly.

Name _____

Monday

1. The last day of skool be finally here.

_____

2. We be helping miss hill put away the books.

_____

Tuesday

1. roy and gene they is leaving school early.

_____

2. they be moveing to alaska.

_____

Wednesday

1. They left oakwood elementary on june 2 2000.

_____

2. they leaved after lunch been over.

_____

Thursday

1. jack and sue was sad to see them leave.

_____

2. lee, jack, and pam was best friends.

_____

Friday

1. they leaved on tuesday at 100 in the afternoon.

_____

2. our vacation will began tomorrow

_____

Week Thirty-Six Answer Key

Corrected Sentences

Skills

		Skills
Monday	1. The last day of school is finally here.	G, S
	2. We are helping Miss Hill put away the books.	C, G
Tuesday	1. Roy and Gene are leaving school early.	C, G
	2. They are moving to Alaska.	C, G, S
Wednesday	1. They left Oakwood Elementary on June 2, 2000.	C, P
	2. They left after lunch was over.	C, G
Thursday	1. Jack and Sue were sad to see them leave.	C, G
	2. Lee, Jack, and Pam were best friends.	C, G
Friday	1. They left on Tuesday at 1:00 in the afternoon.	C, G, P
	2. Our vacation will begin tomorrow.	C, G, P

Assessment One

Name _____

Read each sentence. Study the underlined part. Fill in the circle that corrects the sentence.

Monday

1. <u>mr jones are</u> washing his car now.

   ○ Mr. Jones is
   ○ Mr. jones are
   ○ Mr Jones is
   ○ mr. Jones be

2. <u>tim sayed</u> "I like to run fast."

   ○ Tim sed,
   ○ tim said
   ○ Tim sayed,
   ○ Tim said,

Tuesday

3. <u>may we has</u> a birthday party?

   ○ May we have
   ○ May we has
   ○ may we have
   ○ may we haves

4. <u>joe he seed</u> the bus coming.

   ○ joe seen
   ○ Joe he seed
   ○ Joe seen
   ○ Joe saw

Wednesday

5. When did you <u>get them gloves</u>

   ○ get them gloves?
   ○ get those gloves?
   ○ git those gloves?
   ○ get those gloves.

6. <u>we cant</u> leave yet.

   ○ We ca'nt
   ○ we can't
   ○ We cant
   ○ We can't

Thursday

7. The picnic is <u>friday october 10.</u>

   ○ friday October 10.
   ○ Friday october 10.
   ○ Friday, October 10.
   ○ friday, october, 10.

8. They visited the <u>huntington library</u>

   ○ Huntington Library.
   ○ huntington library.
   ○ huntington Library.
   ○ Huntington library.

Friday

9. <u>my mom pick</u> me up early today.

   ○ My mom pick
   ○ My mom picked
   ○ my mom picked
   ○ My mom she picked

10. <u>ive been work</u> on my homework.

   ○ I be working
   ○ I been working
   ○ I've been working
   ○ I've been work

Assessment covers weeks one and two.

Assessment Two

Name _____

Read each sentence. Study the underlined part. Fill in the circle that corrects the sentence.

Monday

1. The party <u>be on thanksgiving day</u>

   ○ is on Thanksgiving Day
   ○ is on Thanksgiving Day.
   ○ is on thanksgiving day.
   ○ be on Thanksgiving Day.

2. <u>jean ask,</u> "Are you coming?"

   ○ Jean axed,
   ○ Jean ast,
   ○ Jean asked,
   ○ jean asked,

Tuesday

3. <u>he doesnt want</u> to play that game.

   ○ He doesn't want
   ○ he doesn't want
   ○ He doesnt want
   ○ He don't want

4. <u>sue and joe has</u> plans already.

   ○ Sue and Joe has
   ○ Sue and Joe have
   ○ Sue and Joe got
   ○ Sue and joe have

Wednesday

5. <u>me and my dad</u> like to play catch.

   ○ Me and my dad
   ○ My dad and me
   ○ I and my dad
   ○ My dad and I

6. <u>jan she are watch</u> a movie.

   ○ Jan she be watching
   ○ Jan she is watching
   ○ Jan is watching
   ○ Jan are watching

Thursday

7. <u>me and todd likes</u> to swing.

   ○ Me and Todd likes
   ○ Todd and I like
   ○ Todd and me like
   ○ Me and Todd we like

8. <u>i has too</u> brothers.

   ○ I has too
   ○ I have to
   ○ I have two
   ○ I gots two

Friday

9. My uncle lives on <u>lexington street</u>

   ○ lexington street.
   ○ Lexington street.
   ○ Lexington Street
   ○ Lexington Street.

10. The game <u>start at 600</u> tonight.

   ○ starts at 6:00
   ○ starting at 6:00
   ○ start at 6:00
   ○ be starting at 6:00

Assessment covers weeks three and four.

Assessment Three

Name _____

Read each sentence. Study the underlined part. Fill in the circle that corrects the sentence.

Monday

1. <u>ask molly if she be</u> going to sing.

   ○ Ask Molly if she is
   ○ Ask Molly if she be
   ○ Ask molly if she is
   ○ Ask Molly if she

2. The <u>son be shineing</u> brightly today!

   ○ sun is shineing
   ○ son is shining
   ○ sun be shining
   ○ sun is shining

Tuesday

3. <u>leafs be colorful in the fall</u>

   ○ Leafs is colorful in the fall.
   ○ Leaves be colorful in the Fall
   ○ Leafs are colorful in the fall.
   ○ Leaves are colorful in the fall.

4. How many songs <u>dew you no</u>

   ○ do you know?
   ○ do you know
   ○ do you know!
   ○ do you no?

Wednesday

5. <u>Baskitball be my favrite</u> sport.

   ○ Basketball is my favrite
   ○ Basketball be my favorite
   ○ Basketball is my favorite
   ○ Basketball are my favorite

6. <u>lets wach</u> a scary movie!

   ○ Let's wach
   ○ Let's watch
   ○ Lets watch
   ○ Let's wash

Thursday

7. Do you attend <u>westbrook elementary school?</u>

   ○ Westbrook Elementary school?
   ○ Westbrook Elementary School?
   ○ Westbrook Elementary School.
   ○ Westbrook elementary school?

8. Bernie <u>sed, Whats</u> in that basket?"

   ○ said, "Whats
   ○ sayed, "What's
   ○ said, "What's
   ○ said, What's

Friday

9. <u>will you mom cry</u> at the wedding?

   ○ Will your mom cry
   ○ Will your Mom cry
   ○ Will you mom cry
   ○ Will your mom cry?

10. She <u>dont have no</u> money at all.

    ○ doesn't have no
    ○ don't have no
    ○ don't have any
    ○ doesn't have any

78   Assessment covers weeks five and six.   © Carson-Dellosa CD-0042

Assessment Four

Name _____

Read each sentence. Study the underlined part. Fill in the circle that corrects the sentence.

Monday	1. <u>do yer</u> cat like cat food? O Do you O Do your O Does you O Does your	2. <u>walking be</u> more fun than riding. O Walking be O Walking are O Walking is O Walking am
Tuesday	3. The nurse <u>sayed, i will</u> help you." O said, I will O sed, "I will O said, "i will O said, "I will	4. <u>how does</u> you feel today? O How does O How do? O How do O "How do"
Wednesday	5. <u>Arent thanksgiving</u> coming soon? O Isn't Thanksgiving O Aren't Thanksgiving O Isn't thanksgiving O Isnt Thanksgiving	6. <u>i asked mr green</u> for another book. O I asked Mr. green O I asked Mr Green O I ask Mr. Green O I asked Mr. Green
Thursday	7. <u>can you here</u> the dogs barking? O Can you here O Can You hear O Can you hear O Can you hear?	8. Is today <u>wendsday or thursday</u> O Wednesday or Thursday O Wednesday or Thursday? O wednesday or thursday? O Wendsday or Thursday?
Friday	9. Charlie <u>he love to eet</u> pizza. O loves to eet O loves to eat O he loves to eat O he love to eat	10. Do you know <u>mrs katherine taft</u> O Mrs. Katherine Taft? O mrs. Katherine Taft? O Mrs Katherine Taft O Mrs. katherine taft.

Assessment Five

Read each sentence. Study the underlined part. Fill in the circle that corrects the sentence.

Monday	1. Barry said, <u>i have a headache</u> ○ I have a headache ○ I have a headache. ○ "I have a headache." ○ "I have a headache"	2. <u>ill be go</u> to the store with you. ○ I'll be go ○ I'll go ○ I be going ○ I be gone
Tuesday	3. Some <u>peopil dont like</u> vegetables. ○ people don't like ○ people don't likes ○ peopil don't like ○ people they don't like	4. <u>matt and jimmy they be</u> friends. ○ Matt and Jimmy they be ○ Matt and Jimmy are ○ Matt and Jimmy is ○ Matt and jimmy are
Wednesday	5. My favorite month <u>be december</u> ○ be December. ○ is December ○ is December. ○ be december.	6. <u>Skool am</u> a lot of fun! ○ Skool is ○ School am ○ Skool are ○ School is
Thursday	7. Johnny <u>love to ate</u> hot dogs. ○ loves to ate ○ loves to eat ○ love to eat ○ he loves to eat	8. <u>grandmothers name is betty</u> ○ Grandmother's name is Betty. ○ Grandmother's name is betty. ○ Grandmother's name is Betty ○ Grandmothers name is Betty.
Friday	9. <u>where be patty</u> today? ○ where is Patty ○ Where be patty ○ Where is Patty ○ Where is Patty?	10. <u>Whats your fathers name</u> ○ What's your father's name ○ Whats your father's name? ○ What's your fathers name? ○ What's your father's name?

Assessment covers weeks nine and ten.   © Carson-Dellosa CD-0042

Assessment Six

Name _____

Read each sentence. Study the underlined part. Fill in the circle that corrects the sentence.

Monday	1. <u>have anyone seed</u> my bookbag? O Has anyone seen O Has anyone seed O Have anyone seen O Have anyone seed	2. <u>tracy said, "Heres</u> my homework!" O Tracy said, "Here's O Tracy said, "Heres O Tracy said, Here's O tracy said, "Here's
Tuesday	3. <u>isnt today october 11?</u> O Isn't today October 11 O Isnt today October 11? O Isn't today October 11? O Isn't today october 11?	4. Norman <u>he enjoy playing</u> soccer. O enjoy playing O he enjoys playing O "enjoys" playing O enjoys playing
Wednesday	5. <u>we likes</u> to ride in the car. O We likes O We like O We liking O We be liking	6. Virginia <u>have priddy</u> blonde hair. O she have preddy O has priddy O has pretty O have pretty
Thursday	7. <u>don't go swim</u> without a partner. O Doesn't go swim O Dont go swimming O Don't go swimin O Don't go swimming	8. <u>julians dog had</u> puppies last night! O Julian's dog haved O Julian's dog had O Julian's dog it had O Julian's dog having
Friday	9. The <u>cat it falled asleep</u> in my lap. O cat fell asleep O cat it fell asleep O cat falled asleep O Cat fell asleep	10. This <u>be yore new</u> seat. O is your new O be your new O is yore new O is you new

Assessment Seven

Name _____

Read each sentence. Study the underlined part. Fill in the circle that corrects the sentence.

Monday

1. Have you <u>talk to mr thompson?</u>

   ○ talk to Mr. Thompson?
   ○ talked to Mr. Thompson?
   ○ talked to mr. thompson?
   ○ talk to Mr Thompson?

2. <u>what is</u> you doing this weekend?

   ○ What is
   ○ What's are
   ○ what are
   ○ What are

Tuesday

3. Where <u>be 1640 magnolia avenue</u>

   ○ is 1640 Magnolia Avenue?
   ○ is 1640 Magnolia avenue?
   ○ be 1640 Magnolia Avenue?
   ○ are 1640 Magnolia Avenue?

4. Madeline <u>be a vary</u> smart person.

   ○ be a very
   ○ is a very
   ○ is a vary
   ○ are a very

Wednesday

5. <u>jeffs brother is</u> four years old.

   ○ Jeffs brother is
   ○ Jeff's brother he is
   ○ Jeffs brother's
   ○ Jeff's brother is

6. <u>beth and me don't</u> mind staying home.

   ○ Beth and me don't
   ○ I and Beth don't
   ○ Beth and I don't
   ○ Beth and I doesn't

Thursday

7. <u>anne and elliot likes</u> to share.

   ○ Anne and Elliot likes
   ○ Anne and Elliot they like
   ○ Anne and elliot like
   ○ Anne and Elliot like

8. <u>petes mother taked</u> us to watch the new movie.

   ○ Petes mother taked
   ○ Pete's mother took
   ○ Pete's mother taked
   ○ Petes mother took

Friday

9. <u>we dont want no</u> more rainy days.

   ○ We dont want no
   ○ We don't want no
   ○ We don't want any
   ○ We doesn't want any

10. <u>he sed, What is</u> you looking at?"

    ○ He said, "What are
    ○ He said, What are
    ○ He sed, "What is
    ○ He said, "What is

Assessment covers weeks thirteen and fourteen.

Assessment Eight

Name _____

Read each sentence. Study the underlined part. Fill in the circle that corrects the sentence.

Monday

1. <u>i lik to rite</u> with a pencil.

   ○ I lik to write
   ○ I like to right
   ○ I like to rite
   ○ I like to write

2. My name <u>be mr clark</u>

   ○ be Mr. Clark.
   ○ is Mr Clark
   ○ is Mr. Clark.
   ○ is Mr. Clark?

Tuesday

3. Take me to <u>373 east aycock street</u>

   ○ 373 East Aycock Street.
   ○ 373 East Aycock Street
   ○ 373 East Aycock street.
   ○ 373 east Aycock Street.

4. They <u>lives in tulsa oklahoma.</u>

   ○ live in Tulsa Oklahoma.
   ○ live in Tulsa, Oklahoma.
   ○ lives in Tulsa, Oklahoma.
   ○ live in Tulsa, Oklahoma

Wednesday

5. <u>he dont know no</u> magic tricks.

   ○ He dont know no
   ○ He doesn't know no
   ○ He doesn't know any
   ○ He don't know any

6. <u>carol she is a very</u> good reader.

   ○ Carol is a very
   ○ Carol she is a very
   ○ Carol are a very
   ○ Carol be a vary

Thursday

7. <u>delena is learn</u> how to roller skate.

   ○ Delena is learn
   ○ Delena are learning
   ○ Delena she is learning
   ○ Delena is learning

8. <u>eddie and kit they loves</u> to fly kites.

   ○ Eddie and Kit they loves
   ○ Eddie and Kit love
   ○ Eddie and Kit loves
   ○ Eddie and Kit they love

Friday

9. <u>sally she be going</u> to call me later.

   ○ Sally she be going
   ○ Sally going
   ○ Sally she is going
   ○ Sally is going

10. It was cold on <u>october 9 2000</u>

    ○ October 9, 2000
    ○ October 9 2000.
    ○ October 9, 2000.
    ○ October, 9, 2000.

Assessment Nine

Read each sentence. Study the underlined part. Fill in the circle that corrects the sentence.

Monday

1. <u>kim and katie they has</u> a problem.

   - ○ Kim and Katie have
   - ○ Kim and Katie they has
   - ○ Kim and Katie they have
   - ○ Kim and Katie be having

2. They <u>need mr andersons</u> help.

   - ○ needs Mr. Anderson's
   - ○ need Mr. Anderson's
   - ○ need Mr. Andersons
   - ○ need Mr Anderson's

Tuesday

3. We <u>eated turkey on thanksgiving.</u>

   - ○ eated turkey on Thanksgiving.
   - ○ ate turkey on Thanksgiving.
   - ○ eated Turkey on thanksgiving.
   - ○ ate turkey on thanksgiving.

4. <u>dana she have</u> some new friends.

   - ○ Dana she have
   - ○ Dana she has
   - ○ Dana has
   - ○ Dana have

Wednesday

5. I mailed the letter on <u>may 4 2004.</u>

   - ○ May 4 2004.
   - ○ May 4, 2004
   - ○ May, 4, 2004.
   - ○ May 4, 2004.

6. <u>lets surprise erin</u> on her birthday!

   - ○ Let's surprise erin
   - ○ Lets surprise Erin
   - ○ Let's surprise Erin
   - ○ Let's us surprise Erin

Thursday

7. Mom <u>drive us from texas to ohio.</u>

   - ○ drove us from Texas to Ohio.
   - ○ she drove us from Texas to Ohio.
   - ○ drove us from Texas to Ohio
   - ○ drive us from Texas to Ohio.

8. Why <u>dont you rite a letter to he?</u>

   - ○ dont you write a letter to him?
   - ○ don't you write a letter to him?
   - ○ don't you rite a letter to him?
   - ○ don't you write a letter to he?

Friday

9. Have you ever <u>visit atlanta georgia</u>

   - ○ visit Atlanta, Georgia?
   - ○ visited Atlanta, Georgia
   - ○ visited Atlanta, Georgia?
   - ○ visited Atlanta Georgia?

10. Xavier <u>sed, Call me tonite.</u>

    - ○ said, "Call me tonite."
    - ○ said, Call me tonight.
    - ○ sed, "Call me tonight."
    - ○ said, "Call me tonight."

Assessment covers weeks seventeen and eighteen.

Assessment Ten

Name _____

Read each sentence. Study the underlined part. Fill in the circle that corrects the sentence.

Monday

1. <u>me and her cant</u> go to the party.

   - ○ Me and her cant
   - ○ She and I cant
   - ○ Me and her can't
   - ○ She and I can't

2. <u>barry he want</u> a computer for Christmas.

   - ○ Barry wants
   - ○ Barry he want
   - ○ Barry want
   - ○ Barry be wanting

Tuesday

3. Our team <u>are called the oakland bulldogs.</u>

   - ○ are called the Oakland Bulldogs.
   - ○ is called the oakland bulldogs.
   - ○ is called the Oakland Bulldogs.
   - ○ is called the Oakland Bulldogs

4. My neighbor's name <u>are mr fields</u>

   - ○ are Mr Fields
   - ○ are Mr. Fields.
   - ○ is Mr Fields
   - ○ is Mr. Fields.

Wednesday

5. I <u>getted up at 600</u> this morning.

   - ○ getted up at 6:00
   - ○ got up at 600
   - ○ got up at 6:00
   - ○ gotten up at 6:00

6. What time <u>you be comeing over</u>

   - ○ you be comeing over?
   - ○ are you coming over?
   - ○ you be coming over?
   - ○ are you coming over.

Thursday

7. <u>me and jim be</u> watching television.

   - ○ Jim and I are
   - ○ Me and Jim be
   - ○ Me and Jim are
   - ○ Jim and I be

8. <u>kyles birthday is february 8</u>

   - ○ Kyle's birthday is February, 8.
   - ○ Kyle's birthday is february 8.
   - ○ Kyles birthday is February 8.
   - ○ Kyle's birthday is February 8.

Friday

9. We <u>be moveing</u> into a new house!

   - ○ is moveing
   - ○ are moving
   - ○ be moving
   - ○ am moving

10. <u>didnt you think</u> the test was easy?

    - ○ Didnt you think
    - ○ Didnt' you think
    - ○ Didn't you think
    - ○ Didn't you think?

Assessment Eleven

Name _____

Read each sentence. Study the underlined part. Fill in the circle that corrects the sentence.

Monday

1. <u>becky she set</u> quietly in the chair.

   ○ Becky she set
   ○ Becky set
   ○ Becky sat
   ○ Becky she sat

2. We <u>flied from new york to california</u>

   ○ flied from new york to california.
   ○ flied from New York to California.
   ○ flew from New York to California
   ○ flew from New York to California.

Tuesday

3. <u>jason he cant</u> be late another day.

   ○ Jason he cant
   ○ Jason he can't
   ○ Jason cant
   ○ Jason can't

4. <u>bill and tara they has</u> to go home.

   ○ Bill and Tara have
   ○ Bill and Tara they have
   ○ Bill and Tara has
   ○ Bill and Tara they has

Wednesday

5. <u>alice readed</u> us a story yesterday.

   ○ Alice read
   ○ Alice readed
   ○ Alice she read
   ○ Alice reading

6. <u>gordon said, Thats</u> a nice shirt!"

   ○ Gordon said, "Thats
   ○ Gordon said, "That's
   ○ Gordon said, Thats
   ○ Gordon he said, "That's

Thursday

7. <u>where is my</u> gloves, coat, and hat?

   ○ Where is my
   ○ Where are my
   ○ Where be my
   ○ Where are me

8. Weren't you afraid on <u>friday october 13</u>

   ○ on Friday, October, 13?
   ○ on Friday October 13?
   ○ on Friday, October 13?
   ○ on Friday, October 13

Friday

9. We <u>seen mrs phillips</u> at the mall.

   ○ saw mrs Phillips
   ○ seen Mrs Phillips
   ○ saw Mrs. Phillips
   ○ seen Mrs. Phillips

10. <u>bob he said,</u> "Wait for me!"

   ○ Bob he said,
   ○ Bob sayed
   ○ Bob sayed,
   ○ Bob said,

Assessment covers weeks twenty-one and twenty-two.

Assessment Twelve

Name _____

Read each sentence. Study the underlined part. Fill in the circle that corrects the sentence.

Monday

1. We're going to <u>kansas next june</u>

   ○ kansas next june.
   ○ kansas next June.
   ○ Kansas next June.
   ○ Kansas next june.

2. Todd <u>drawed a picture of mr pines</u>

   ○ drawed a picture of Mr. Pines
   ○ drew a picture of mr. Pines.
   ○ drew a picture of Mr. Pines.
   ○ drawn a picture of Mr. Pines.

Tuesday

3. <u>chris and me thinks</u> it is too cold.

   ○ Chris and I think
   ○ Chris and I thinks
   ○ Me and Chris think
   ○ Me and Chris we think

4. Have you ever <u>seen the pacific ocean</u>

   ○ seen the pacific ocean?
   ○ seen the Pacific Ocean?
   ○ saw the Pacific Ocean?
   ○ seen the Pacific ocean?

Wednesday

5. <u>miss perez she like</u> to sing.

   ○ Miss Perez she like
   ○ Miss Perez she likes
   ○ Miss Perez likes
   ○ Miss Perez like

6. <u>isnt that wendys</u> backpack?

   ○ Isnt that Wendy's
   ○ Isn't that Wendys
   ○ Isn't that Wendy's?
   ○ Isn't that Wendy's

Thursday

7. Henry <u>he get on the bus at 700.</u>

   ○ gets on the bus at 7:00.
   ○ he gets on the bus at 7:00.
   ○ get on the bus at 7:00.
   ○ gets on the bus at 7:00

8. <u>jeff and misty they runned</u> home.

   ○ Jeff and Misty they runned
   ○ Jeff and Misty ran
   ○ Jeff and Misty they ran
   ○ Jeff and Misty runned

Friday

9. The <u>fourth of july be</u> very exciting!

   ○ Fourth of July be
   ○ fourth of July be
   ○ Fourth of july are
   ○ Fourth of July is

10. Doug said, <u>Lets get reddy</u> to go!"

    ○ Let's get reddy
    ○ Let's get ready
    ○ "Let's get ready
    ○ "Lets get ready

Assessment Thirteen

Name _____

Read each sentence. Study the underlined part. Fill in the circle that corrects the sentence.

Monday

1. <u>Are frends is playing</u> in the yard.

   O Our friends are playing
   O Are friends are playing
   O Our friends is playing
   O Our frends playing

2. <u>me and ricky wants</u> to be artists.

   O Me and Ricky wants
   O Ricky and I want
   O Ricky and I wants
   O Me and Ricky want

Tuesday

3. My sister <u>she cant eat no</u> candy.

   O she can't eat no
   O can't eat no
   O can't eat any
   O she can't eat any

4. <u>derek sed, im</u> going home now."

   O Derek sed, I'm
   O Derek said, "Im
   O Derek said, "I'm
   O Derek said, I'm

Wednesday

5. <u>abby sed, i hope lucy</u> can visit us this weekend."

   O Abby sed, "I hope Lucy
   O Abby said, "I hope Lucy
   O Abby said, "I hope lucy
   O Abby said, I hope Lucy

6. <u>wheres my new toothbrush</u>

   O Where's my new toothbrush
   O Wheres my new toothbrush?
   O Where's mi nue toothbrush?
   O Where's my new toothbrush?

Thursday

7. Candice <u>she be over their</u>

   O is over there.
   O she is over there.
   O be over their.
   O is over their.

8. Have you ever <u>visit alaska or hawaii</u>

   O visit Alaska or Hawaii
   O visit Alaska or Hawaii?
   O visited alaska or hawaii?
   O visited Alaska or Hawaii?

Friday

9. Isn't that <u>howse on high point road</u>

   O house on High Point road.
   O howse on High Point Road
   O house on High Point Road?
   O howse on high point Road?

10. What <u>happen on july 4 1776</u>

   O happen on July 4, 1776?
   O happened on July 4, 1776?
   O happened on july 4 1776?
   O happen on July, 4, 1776.

Assessment covers weeks twenty-five and twenty-six.

Assessment Fourteen

Name _____

Read each sentence. Study the underlined part. Fill in the circle that corrects the sentence.

Monday

1. <u>juans father be</u> smart and friendly.

   ○ Juan's father be
   ○ Juan's father is
   ○ Juan his father is
   ○ Juan's father are

2. <u>me and tony be</u> on the same team.

   ○ Tony and I are
   ○ Tony and me are
   ○ Me and Tony are
   ○ I and Tony be

Tuesday

3. <u>dr allen gived</u> her some medicine.

   ○ Dr. Allen gived
   ○ Dr Allen give
   ○ Dr. allen gave
   ○ Dr. Allen gave

4. Karen <u>were absent thursday</u>

   ○ were absent thursday?
   ○ was absent Thursday
   ○ was absent Thursday.
   ○ been absent Thursday.

Wednesday

5. <u>your my bestest frend!</u>

   ○ You're my best friend!
   ○ You're my bestest frend!
   ○ Your my best friend!
   ○ You my best friend!

6. <u>bills birthday isnt</u> until December.

   ○ Bill's birthday isnt
   ○ Bills birthday isn't
   ○ Bill's birthday isn't
   ○ Bill's birthday aren't

Thursday

7. <u>vicky she hasnt</u> been here long.

   ○ Vicky she hasnt
   ○ Vicky hasn't
   ○ Vicky she hasn't
   ○ Vicky haven't

8. They <u>move on march 8 2001.</u>

   ○ moved on March 8, 2001.
   ○ moved on March 8 2001.
   ○ move on March 8, 2001.
   ○ moved on March, 8, 2001.

Friday

9. <u>ill met you by that tree at 430</u>

   ○ I'll met you by that tree at 4:30.
   ○ I'll meet you by that tree at 4:30.
   ○ Ill meet you by that tree at 4:30.
   ○ I'll meet you by that tree at 430.

10. <u>me and jan rided</u> bikes yesterday.

   ○ Me and Jan rided
   ○ Me and Jan rode
   ○ Jan and I rode
   ○ Jan and I rided

Assessment Fifteen

Name _____

Read each sentence. Study the underlined part. Fill in the circle that corrects the sentence.

Monday

1. <u>wear did i</u> put my pencil?

   ○ Wear did I
   ○ Wear did i
   ○ Where did I
   ○ Where I

2. <u>on may 7 2002,</u> we will have a book sale.

   ○ On May, 7, 2002,
   ○ On may 7, 2002,
   ○ On May 7 2002,
   ○ On May 7, 2002,

Tuesday

3. It <u>were relly nice to see dr madison.</u>

   ○ were really nice to see Dr. Madison.
   ○ was relly nice to see Dr. Madison.
   ○ was really nice to see Dr. Madison.
   ○ was really nise to see Dr Madison?

4. The first bell <u>it ring at 805</u>

   ○ rings at 8:05.
   ○ it ring at 8:05.
   ○ rings at 805
   ○ ringing at 8:05.

Wednesday

5. <u>jane sayed, that</u> paper is mine."

   ○ Jane said, "That
   ○ Jane said, That
   ○ Jane sayed, "That
   ○ jane said, "That

6. <u>aunt emmy finded</u> my lost cards.

   ○ Aunt Emmy finded
   ○ Aunt Emmy found
   ○ Aunt Emmy she found
   ○ Aunt Emmy find

Thursday

7. <u>mr larsen didnt</u> see us arrive.

   ○ Mr. larsen didn't
   ○ Mr. Larsen didn't
   ○ Mr Larsen didn't
   ○ Mr. Larsen didnt

8. I met <u>she on sunday, may 6 2001.</u>

   ○ she on Sunday, May 6, 2001.
   ○ her on Sunday, May, 6, 2001.
   ○ her on "Sunday, May 6, 2001."
   ○ her on Sunday, May 6, 2001.

Friday

9. How long <u>be the mississippi river</u>

   ○ be the mississippi river?
   ○ are the Mississippi River?
   ○ is the Mississippi River.
   ○ is the Mississippi River?

10. <u>garys dog isnt</u> very large.

    ○ Gary's dog aren't
    ○ Garys dog isn't
    ○ Gary's dog isnt
    ○ Gary's dog isn't

Assessment covers weeks twenty-nine and thirty.

Assessment Sixteen

Name _____

Read each sentence. Study the underlined part. Fill in the circle that corrects the sentence.

Monday	1. <u>mr stewart he give</u> me a book to read. ○ Mr. Stewart he give ○ Mr. Stewart he gave ○ Mr. Stewart give ○ Mr. Stewart gave	2. My book <u>be call</u> *The Great Idea.* ○ be called ○ are call ○ is called ○ it is called
Tuesday	3. She'll be <u>in miami until wendsdy</u> ○ in Miami until Wendsdy. ○ in miami until Wednesday. ○ in Miami until Wednesday ○ in Miami until Wednesday.	4. The football game <u>begin at 700</u> ○ it begin at 7:00 ○ beginning at 700. ○ begins at 7:00. ○ is begin at 7:00.
Wednesday	5. The bus <u>stop at 205 north main street.</u> ○ stop at 205 North Main Street. ○ stopped at 205 North Main Street. ○ stopped at 205 north Main street. ○ stopped at 205 North Main Street	6. <u>doug and aaron they fix</u> the problem. ○ Doug and Aaron they fix ○ Doug and Aaron fixed ○ Doug and aaron fixed ○ Doug and Aaron fix
Thursday	7. <u>mrs ellis she come</u> to visit today. ○ Mrs. Ellis came ○ Mrs. Ellis she come ○ Mrs. Ellis she came ○ Mrs. ellis came	8. <u>mandy ask, Whats</u> in the bag?" ○ Mandy ask, "What's ○ Mandy ask, "Whats ○ Mandy asked, "What's ○ Mandy she asked, "What's
Friday	9. <u>its to late to</u> get started now. ○ It's too late to ○ Its too late to ○ It's to late too ○ Its to late too	10. <u>why dont we try agin</u> tomorrow? ○ Why don't we try agin ○ Why dont we try again ○ Why don't we try again ○ Why doesn't we try again

Assessment Seventeen

Name _____

Read each sentence. Study the underlined part. Fill in the circle that corrects the sentence.

Monday

1. I <u>cant wait until 315 today!</u>

   - ○ can't wait until 315 today!
   - ○ can't wait until 3:15 today!
   - ○ cant wait until 3:15 today!
   - ○ can't waiting until 3:15 today!

2. We watch that show <u>ever mondy nite!</u>

   - ○ ever Monday night!
   - ○ every Monday night!
   - ○ every monday night!
   - ○ every Mondy night!

Tuesday

3. Did it <u>rained more in april or may</u>

   - ○ rained more in April or May?
   - ○ rain more in April or May?
   - ○ rain more in April or May.
   - ○ "rain more in April or May?"

4. Julie <u>she live on andover avenue</u>

   - ○ she live on Andover Avenue.
   - ○ live on Andover Avenue.
   - ○ lives on Andover Avenue.
   - ○ be living on Andover Avenue.

Wednesday

5. Will you call me <u>saturday at 500</u>

   - ○ Saturday at 5:00?
   - ○ saterday at 5:00?
   - ○ Saturday at 500?
   - ○ Saterday at 5:00.

6. <u>mr and mrs carson likes</u> to travel.

   - ○ Mr. and Mrs. Carson likes
   - ○ Mr. and Mrs. carson like
   - ○ Mr and Mrs Carson like
   - ○ Mr. and Mrs. Carson like

Thursday

7. <u>me and amber want</u> a new puppy.

   - ○ Me and Amber want
   - ○ I and Amber want
   - ○ Amber and me wants
   - ○ Amber and I want

8. They <u>be moveing to maryland</u>

   - ○ be moveing to Maryland.
   - ○ are moving to maryland
   - ○ are moving to Maryland.
   - ○ is moving to Maryland.

Friday

9. I <u>dont have no more</u> questions.

   - ○ don't have any more
   - ○ don't have no more
   - ○ ain't got no more
   - ○ don't got any more

10. Mom asked, <u>Wheres Kims hat?</u>

   - ○ "Where's Kim hat?
   - ○ "Where's kim's hat?"
   - ○ "Where's Kim's hat?"
   - ○ "Wheres Kims hat?"

Assessment covers weeks thirty-three and thirty-four.

Assessment Eighteen

Name _____

Read each sentence. Study the underlined part. Fill in the circle that corrects the sentence.

Monday

1. Is Mr. Alva's address <u>41 south jefferson street</u>

   O 41 south jefferson street?
   O 41 south Jefferson street.
   O 41 South Jefferson Street
   O 41 South Jefferson Street?

2. <u>i and jill we play</u> ball at recess.

   O Jill and I play
   O I and Jill we play
   O Jill and me play
   O Me and Jill play

Tuesday

3. <u>is mr read</u> helping you today?

   O Is Mr Read
   O Is Mr. Read?
   O Is Mr. read
   O Is Mr. Read

4. <u>mom said, dont</u> forget your coat."

   O Mom said, "Don't
   O Mom said, "Dont
   O mom said, "Don't
   O Mom said, Don't

Wednesday

5. The movie <u>last from 700 until 830.</u>

   O last from 7:00 until 8:30.
   O it lasts from 7:00 until 8:30.
   O lasts from 700 until 830.
   O lasts from 7:00 until 8:30.

6. Darren <u>miss the bus last friday.</u>

   O miss the bus last Friday.
   O missed the bus last Friday.
   O missed the bus last friday.
   O missed the bus last Friday

Thursday

7. <u>scott ask, wheres</u> my pencil?"

   O Scott asked, "Where's
   O Scott asked, "Where
   O Scott he ask, "Where's
   O Scott ask, "Where's

8. He asked, <u>was you home saturday</u>

   O Was you home Saturday?
   O Were you home Saturday?
   O "Were you home Saturday?"
   O "Was you home Saturday?"

Friday

9. Do you remember <u>monday, december 25 2000</u>

   O monday, december 25, 2000?
   O Monday December 25 2000?
   O Monday, December 25, 2000?
   O Monday, December 25, 2000.

10. <u>i has a dog name festus</u>

    O I has a dog named Festus.
    O I have a dog named Festus.
    O I have a dog named festus.
    O I have a dog name Festus.

Assessment covers weeks thirty-five and thirty-six.

Assessment Answer Key

p. 76 Assessment 1

Monday
1. mr jones are washing his car now.
   - ● Mr. Jones is
   - ○ Mr. Jones are
   - ○ Mr. Jones is
   - ○ mr. Jones be
2. tim sayed "I like to run fast."
   - ○ Tim sed,
   - ○ tim said
   - ○ Tim sayed,
   - ● Tim said,

Tuesday
3. may we has a birthday party?
   - ● May we have
   - ○ May we has
   - ○ may we have
   - ○ may we haves
4. joe he seed the bus coming.
   - ○ joe seen
   - ○ Joe he seed
   - ○ Joe seen
   - ● Joe saw

Wednesday
5. When did you get them gloves
   - ○ get them gloves?
   - ● get those gloves?
   - ○ gif those gloves?
   - ○ get those gloves.
6. we cant leave yet.
   - ○ We ca'nt
   - ○ we can't
   - ● We can't
   - ○ We can't

Thursday
7. The picnic is friday october 10.
   - ○ friday October 10.
   - ○ Friday october 10.
   - ● Friday, October 10.
   - ○ friday, october. 10.
8. They visited the huntington library.
   - ● Huntington Library.
   - ○ huntington library.
   - ○ Huntington Library.
   - ○ Huntington library.

Friday
9. ive been work on my homework.
   - ○ I be working
   - ○ I been working
   - ● I've been working
   - ○ I've been work
10. my mom pick me up early today.
   - ○ My mom pick
   - ○ My mom picked
   - ● my mom picked
   - ○ My mom she picked

p. 77 Assessment 2

Monday
1. The party be on thanksgiving day
   - ● is on Thanksgiving Day
   - ○ is on Thanksgiving Day.
   - ○ is on Thanksgiving Day.
   - ○ be on Thanksgiving Day.
2. jean ask, "Are you coming?"
   - ○ Jean axed,
   - ○ Jean ast,
   - ● Jean asked,
   - ○ Jean asked.

Tuesday
3. he doesnt want to play that game.
   - ○ He doesn't want
   - ● He doesn't want
   - ○ He doesnt want
   - ○ He don't want

4. sue and joe has plans already.
   - ○ Sue and Joe has
   - ○ Sue and Joe have
   - ● Sue and Joe got
   - ○ Sue and Joe have

Wednesday
5. me and my dad like to play catch.
   - ○ Me and my dad
   - ○ My dad and me
   - ○ I and my dad
   - ● My dad and I
6. jan she are watch a movie.
   - ○ Jan she be watching
   - ○ Jan she watching
   - ● Jan is watching
   - ○ Jan are watching

Thursday
7. me and todd likes to swing.
   - ○ Me and Todd likes
   - ● Todd and I like
   - ○ Todd and me like
   - ○ Me and Todd we like
8. i has too brothers.
   - ○ I has too
   - ● I have two
   - ○ I have two
   - ○ I gots two

Friday
9. My uncle lives on lexington street
   - ○ lexington street.
   - ● Lexington Street.
   - ○ Lexington street.
   - ○ Lexington Street.
10. The game start at 6:00 tonight.
    - ○ starts at 6:00
    - ○ starting at 6:00
    - ● start at 6:00
    - ○ be starting at 6:00

p. 78 Assessment 3

Monday
1. ask molly if she be going to sing.
   - ○ Ask Molly if she is
   - ● Ask Molly if she be
   - ○ Ask molly if she is
   - ○ Ask Molly if she
2. The son be shineing brightly today!
   - ○ sun is shineing
   - ○ son is shining
   - ● sun is shining
   - ○ sun is shining

Tuesday
3. leafs be colorful in the fall
   - ○ Leafs is colorful in the fall.
   - ○ Leaves be colorful in the Fall.
   - ○ Leafs are colorful in the fall.
   - ● Leaves are colorful in the fall.
4. How many songs dew you no
   - ● do you know?
   - ○ do you know
   - ○ do you know!
   - ○ do you no?

Wednesday
5. Basketball be my favorite sport.
   - ○ Basketball is my favorite
   - ● Basketball be my favorite
   - ○ Basketball is my favorite
   - ○ Basketball are my favorite
6. lets watch a scary movie!
   - ● Let's watch
   - ○ Let's watch
   - ○ Lets watch
   - ○ Let's wash

Thursday
7. Do you attend westbrook elementary school?
   - ○ Westbrook Elementary school?
   - ○ Westbrook Elementary School.
   - ● Westbrook Elementary School?
   - ○ Westbrook elementary school?
8. Bernie sed, Whats in that basket?"
   - ○ said, "Whats
   - ○ sayed, "What's
   - ● said, "What's
   - ○ said, What's

Friday
9. will you mom cry at the wedding?
   - ○ Will your mom cry
   - ○ Will your Mom cry
   - ● Will you mom cry
   - ○ Will your mom cry?
10. She dont have no money at all.
    - ○ doesn't have no
    - ○ don't have no
    - ○ don't have any
    - ● doesn't have any

p. 79 Assessment 4

Monday
1. do yer cat like cat food?
   - ○ Do you
   - ○ Do your
   - ● Does you
   - ○ Does your
2. walking be more fun than riding.
   - ○ Walking be
   - ○ Walking are
   - ● Walking is
   - ○ Walking am

Tuesday
3. The nurse sayed, I will help you."
   - ● said, I will
   - ○ sed, "I will
   - ○ said, "I will
   - ○ said, "I will
4. how does you feel today?
   - ○ How does
   - ○ How do?
   - ● How do
   - ○ "How do"

Wednesday
5. Arent thanksgiving coming soon?
   - ○ Isn't Thanksgiving
   - ○ Aren't Thanksgiving
   - ● Isn't thanksgiving
   - ○ Isnt Thanksgiving
6. I asked mr green for another book.
   - ○ I asked Mr. green
   - ○ I asked Mr Green
   - ○ I ask Mr. Green
   - ● I asked Mr. Green

Thursday
7. can you here the dogs barking?
   - ○ Can you here
   - ● Can You hear
   - ○ Can you hear
   - ○ Can you hear?
8. Is today wendsday or thursday?
   - ○ Wednesday or Thursday
   - ● Wednesday or Thursday?
   - ○ wednesday or thursday?
   - ○ Wendsday or Thursday?

Friday
9. Charlie he love to eat pizza.
   - ● loves to eat
   - ○ loves to eat
   - ○ he loves to eat
   - ○ he love to eat
10. Do you know miss katherine taft
    - ● Mrs. Katherine Taft?
    - ○ mrs. Katherine Taft?
    - ○ Mrs. Katherine Taft
    - ○ Mrs. katherine taft.

p. 80 Assessment 5

Monday
1. Barry said, I have a headache
   - ○ I have a headache
   - ● I have a headache.
   - ○ "I have a headache."
   - ○ "I have a headache"
2. Ill be go to the store with you.
   - ○ I'll be go
   - ○ I'll go
   - ● I be going
   - ○ I be gone

Tuesday
3. Some peopil dont like vegetables.
   - ○ people don't like
   - ○ people don't likes
   - ● peopil don't like
   - ○ people they don't like
4. matt and jimmy they be friends.
   - ○ Matt and Jimmy they be
   - ● Matt and Jimmy are
   - ○ Matt and Jimmy is
   - ○ Matt and Jimmy are

Wednesday
5. My favorite month be december
   - ○ be December.
   - ● is December.
   - ○ is December
   - ○ be december.
6. Skool am a lot of fun!
   - ○ Skool is
   - ○ School am
   - ○ Skool are
   - ● School is

Thursday
7. Johnny love to ate hot dogs.
   - ○ loves to ate
   - ○ loves to eat
   - ● love to eat
   - ○ he loves to eat
8. grandmothers name is betty
   - ○ Grandmother's name is Betty.
   - ○ Grandmother's name is betty
   - ● Grandmother's name is Betty
   - ○ Grandmother's name is Betty.

Friday
9. where is patty today?
   - ○ where is Patty
   - ● Where be patty?
   - ○ Where is Patty
   - ○ Where is Patty?
10. Whats your fathers name
    - ○ What's your father's name
    - ○ Whats your father's name?
    - ○ What's your fathers name?
    - ● What's your father's name?

p. 81 Assessment 6

Monday
1. have anyone seed my bookbag?
   - ● Has anyone seen
   - ○ Has anyone seed
   - ○ Have anyone seen
   - ○ Have anyone seed
2. tracy said, "Heres my homework!"
   - ● Tracy said, "Here's
   - ○ Tracy said, "Heres
   - ○ Tracy said, Here's
   - ○ tracy said, "Here's

Tuesday
3. isnt today october 11?
   - ● Isn't today October 11
   - ○ Isnt today October 11?
   - ○ Isn't today October 11?
   - ○ Isn't today october 11?
4. Norman he enjoy playing soccer.
   - ○ enjoy playing
   - ○ he enjoys playing
   - ○ "enjoys" playing
   - ● enjoys playing

Wednesday
5. we likes to ride in the car.
   - ● We likes
   - ○ We like
   - ○ We liking
   - ○ We be liking
6. Virginia have priddy blonde hair.
   - ○ she have preddy
   - ○ has priddy
   - ● has pretty
   - ○ have pretty

Thursday
7. dont go swim without a partner.
   - ○ Doesn't go swim
   - ○ Don't go swimming
   - ○ Don't go swimin
   - ● Don't go swimming
8. Julians dog had puppies last night!
   - ● Julian's dog haved
   - ○ Julian's dog had
   - ○ Julian's dog it had
   - ○ Julian's dog having

Friday
9. The cat it falled asleep in my lap.
   - ● cat fell asleep
   - ○ cat it fell asleep
   - ○ cat falled asleep
   - ○ Cat fell asleep
10. This be yore new seat.
    - ● is your new
    - ○ be your new
    - ○ is yore new
    - ○ is you new

Assessment Answer Key

p. 82 Assessment 7

Monday
1. Have you talk to mr thompson?
   - ● talk to Mr. Thompson?
   - ○ talked to Mr. Thompson?
   - ○ talked to mr. thompson?
   - ○ talk to Mr Thompson?
2. what is you doing this weekend?
   - ○ What is
   - ○ What's are
   - ○ what are
   - ● What are

Tuesday
3. Where be 1640 magnolia avenue
   - ○ Is 1640 Magnolia Avenue?
   - ○ Is 1640 Magnolia avenue?
   - ● be 1640 Magnolia Avenue?
   - ○ are 1640 Magnolia Avenue?
4. Madeline be a vary smart person.
   - ○ be a very
   - ○ is a very
   - ● is a vary
   - ○ are a very

Wednesday
5. Jeffs brother is four years old.
   - ● Jeffs brother is
   - ○ Jeff's brother he is
   - ○ Jeffs brother's
   - ○ Jeff' brother is
6. beth and me don't mind staying home.
   - ○ Beth and me and don't
   - ○ I and Beth don't
   - ● Beth and I don't
   - ○ Beth and I doesn't

Thursday
7. anne and elliot likes to share.
   - ○ Anne and Elliot likes
   - ○ Anne and Elliot they like
   - ● Anne and elliot like
   - ○ Anne and Elliot like
8. petes mother taked us to watch the new movie.
   - ● Petes mother taked
   - ○ Pete's mother took
   - ○ Pete's mother taked
   - ○ Petes mother took

Friday
9. we don't want no more rainy days.
   - ○ We dont want no
   - ○ We don't want no
   - ● We don't want any
   - ○ We doesn't want any
10. he sed, What is you looking at?"
    - ● He said, "What are
    - ○ He said, What are
    - ○ He said, "What is
    - ○ He sed, "What is

p. 83 Assessment 8

Monday
1. I lik to rite with a pencil.
   - ○ I like to write
   - ○ I like to right
   - ○ I like to rite
   - ● I like to write
2. My name be mr clark
   - ○ be Mr. Clark.
   - ○ Is Mr Clark
   - ● Is Mr. Clark.
   - ○ is Mr. Clark?

Tuesday
3. Take me to 373 east aycock street
   - ● 373 East Aycock Street.
   - ○ 373 East Aycock Street
   - ○ 373 east Aycock street.
   - ○ 373 east Aycock Street,
4. They lives in tulsa oklahoma.
   - ○ live in Tulsa Oklahoma.
   - ○ live in Tulsa, Oklahoma.
   - ● lives in Tulsa, Oklahoma.
   - ○ live in Tulsa, Oklahoma

Wednesday
5. carol she is a very good reader.
   - ● Carol is a very
   - ○ Carol she is a very
   - ○ Carol are a very
   - ○ Carol be a very
6. he dont know no magic tricks.
   - ○ He dont know no
   - ○ He doesn't know no
   - ● He doesn't know any
   - ○ He don't know any

Thursday
7. delena is learn how to roller skate.
   - ○ Delena is learn
   - ○ Delena are learning
   - ● Delena is learning
   - ○ Delena is learning
8. eddie and kit they loves to fly kites.
   - ○ Eddie and Kit they loves
   - ○ Eddie and Kit love
   - ● Eddie and Kit love
   - ○ Eddie and Kit they love

Friday
9. sally she be going to call me later.
   - ○ Sally she be going
   - ○ Sally going
   - ● Sally she is going
   - ○ Sally she is going
10. It was cold on october 9 2000
    - ○ October 9, 2000
    - ○ October 9 2000.
    - ○ October 9, 2000.
    - ● October, 9, 2000.

p. 84 Assessment 9

Monday
1. kim and katie they has a problem.
   - ● Kim and Katie have
   - ○ Kim and Katie they has
   - ○ Kim and Katie they have
   - ○ Kim and Katie be having
2. They need mr andersons help.
   - ● needs Mr. Anderson's
   - ○ need Mr. Anderson's
   - ○ need Mr. Andersons
   - ○ need Mr Anderson's

Tuesday
3. We eated turkey on thanksgiving.
   - ○ eated turkey on Thanksgiving.
   - ● ate turkey on Thanksgiving.
   - ○ eated Turkey on thanksgiving.
   - ○ ate turkey on thanksgiving.
4. dana she have some new friends.
   - ○ Dana she have
   - ● Dana she has
   - ○ Dana has
   - ○ Dana have

Wednesday
5. I mailed the letter on may 4 2004.
   - ○ May 4 2004.
   - ● May 4, 2004.
   - ○ May, 4, 2004.
   - ○ May 4, 2004,
6. lets surprise erin on her birthday!
   - ● Let's surprise erin
   - ○ Lets surprise Erin
   - ○ Let's surprise Erin
   - ○ Let' us surprise Erin

Thursday
7. Mom drive us from texas to ohio.
   - ○ drive us from Texas to Ohio.
   - ○ she drove us from Texas to Ohio.
   - ● drove us from Texas to Ohio.
   - ○ drive us from Texas to Ohio.
8. Why dont you rite a letter to he?
   - ○ dont you write a letter to him?
   - ● don't you write a letter to him?
   - ○ don't you rite a letter to him?
   - ○ don't you write a letter to he?

Friday
9. Have you ever visit atlanta georgia
   - ○ visit Atlanta, Georgia?
   - ● visited Atlanta, Georgia
   - ○ visited Atlanta, Georgia?
   - ○ visited Atlanta Georgia?
10. Xavier sed, Call me tonite.
    - ○ said, "Call me tonite."
    - ○ said, Call me tonight.
    - ○ sed, "Call me tonight."
    - ● said, "Call me tonight!"

p. 85 Assessment 10

Monday
1. me and her cant go to the party.
   - ● Me and her can't
   - ○ She and I cant
   - ○ Me and her can't
   - ○ She and I can't
2. barry he want a computer for Christmas.
   - ● Barry wants
   - ○ Barry he want
   - ○ Barry want
   - ○ Barry be wanting

Tuesday
3. Our team are called the oakland bulldogs.
   - ○ are called the Oakland Bulldogs.
   - ○ are called the oakland bulldogs.
   - ● is called the Oakland Bulldogs.
   - ○ is called the Oakland Bulldogs
4. My neighbor's name are mr fields.
   - ○ are Mr Fields
   - ○ are Mr. Fields.
   - ○ is Mr Fields
   - ● is Mr. Fields.

Wednesday
5. I getted up at 600 this morning.
   - ○ getted up at 6:00
   - ● got up at 6:00
   - ○ got up at 6:00
   - ○ gotten up at 6:00
6. What time you be comeing over?
   - ○ you be coming over?
   - ● you be coming over?
   - ○ you be coming over?
   - ○ are you coming over.

Thursday
7. me and jim is watching television.
   - ○ Jim and I are
   - ● Me and Jim be
   - ○ Me and Jim be
   - ○ Jim and I be
8. kyles birthday is february 8
   - ○ Kyle's birthday is February, 8.
   - ● Kyle's birthday is february 8.
   - ○ Kyle's birthday is February 8.
   - ○ Kyle's birthday is February 8.

Friday
9. We be moveing into a new house!
   - ○ is moveing
   - ○ are moving
   - ● be moving
   - ○ am moving
10. didnt you think the test was easy?
    - ● Didnt you think
    - ○ Didn' you think
    - ○ Didn't you think
    - ○ Didn't you think?

p. 86 Assessment 11

Monday
1. becky she set quietly in the chair.
   - ○ Becky she set
   - ● Becky set
   - ○ Becky sat
   - ○ Becky she sat
2. We flied from new york to california.
   - ○ flied from New York to California.
   - ● flied from New York to California.
   - ○ flew from New York to California.
   - ○ flew from New York to California.

Tuesday
3. Jason he cant be late another day.
   - ○ Jason he cant
   - ○ Jason he can't
   - ○ Jason cant
   - ● Jason can't
4. bill and tara they has to go home.
   - ○ Bill and Tara have
   - ● Bill and Tara they have
   - ○ Bill and Tara has
   - ○ Bill and Tara they has

Wednesday
5. alice readed us a story yesterday.
   - ● Alice read
   - ○ Alice readed
   - ○ Alice she read
   - ○ Alice reading
6. gordon said, Thats a nice shirt!"
   - ○ Gordon said, "That's
   - ● Gordon said, "That's
   - ○ Gordon she read "That's
   - ○ Gordon he said, "That's

Thursday
7. where is my gloves, coat, and hat?
   - ○ Where are my
   - ● Where are my
   - ○ Where be my
   - ○ Where are me
8. Weren't you afraid on friday october 13
   - ○ on Friday, October, 13?
   - ○ on Friday, October 13?
   - ● on Friday, October 13?
   - ○ on Friday, October 13

Friday
9. We seen mrs phillips at the mall.
   - ○ saw mrs Phillips
   - ○ seen Mrs Phillips
   - ● saw Mrs. Phillips
   - ○ seen Mrs. Phillips
10. bob he said, Wait for me!"
    - ○ Bob he said.
    - ○ Bob sayed,
    - ● Bob sayed,
    - ○ Bob said.

p. 87 Assessment 12

Monday
1. We're going to kansas next june.
   - ○ kansas next June.
   - ○ kansas next june.
   - ● Kansas next June.
   - ○ Kansas next june.
2. Todd drawed a picture of mr pines
   - ○ drawed a picture of Mr. Pines
   - ● drew a picture of mr. Pines.
   - ○ drew a picture of Mr. Pines.
   - ○ drawn a picture of Mr. Pines.

Tuesday
3. chris and me thinks it is too cold.
   - ○ Chris and I think
   - ○ Chris and I thinks
   - ● Me and Chris think
   - ○ Me and Chris we think
4. Have you ever seen the pacific ocean
   - ○ seen the pacific ocean?
   - ● seen the Pacific Ocean?
   - ○ seen the Pacific Ocean?
   - ○ seen the Pacific ocean?

Wednesday
5. miss perez she like to sing.
   - ○ Miss Perez she like
   - ● Miss Perez she likes
   - ○ Miss Perez likes
   - ○ Miss Perez like
6. isnt that wendys backpack?
   - ○ Isn't that Wendy's
   - ● Isn't that Wendys
   - ○ Isn't that Wendy's?
   - ○ Isn't that Wendy's

Thursday
7. Henry he get on the bus at 700.
   - ○ gets on the bus at 7:00.
   - ● he gets on the bus at 7:00.
   - ○ get on the bus at 7:00.
   - ○ gets on the bus at 7:00
8. jeff and misty they runned home.
   - ○ Jeff and Misty they ran
   - ● Jeff and Misty ran
   - ○ Jeff and Misty they ran
   - ○ Jeff and Misty runned

Friday
9. The fourth of july be very exciting!
   - ○ Fourth of July be
   - ○ fourth of july be
   - ● Fourth of July are
   - ○ Fourth of July is
10. Doug said, Lets get reddy to go!"
    - ○ Let's get reddy
    - ○ Let's get ready
    - ● "Let's get ready
    - ○ "Lets get ready

Assessment Answer Key

p. 88 Assessment 13

Monday
1. Are friends is playing in the yard.
   - ○ Our friends are playing
   - ○ Are friends are playing
   - ○ Our friends is playing
   - ● Our frends playing
2. me and ricky wants to be artists.
   - ○ Me and Ricky wants
   - ● Ricky and I want
   - ○ Ricky and I wants
   - ○ Me and Ricky want

Tuesday
3. My sister she can't eat no candy.
   - ○ she can't eat no
   - ○ can't eat no
   - ● can't eat any
   - ○ she can't eat any
4. derek sed, I'm going home now."
   - ○ Derek sed, I'm
   - ○ Dr Allen give
   - ● Derek said. "I'm
   - ○ Derek said, I'm

Wednesday
5. abby said, I hope Lucy can visit us this weekend."
   - ● Abby said, "I hope Lucy
   - ○ Abby sed, "I hope Lucy
   - ○ Abby said, "I'm hope Lucy
   - ○ Abby said, I hope Lucy
6. wheres my new toothbrush?
   - ○ Where's my new toothbrush?
   - ● Wheres my new toothbrush?
   - ○ Where's mi nue toothbrush?
   - ○ Where's my new toothbrush?

Thursday
7. Have you ever visit alaska or hawaii
   - ○ visit Alaska or Hawaii
   - ● visit Alaska or Hawaii?
   - ○ visited alaska or hawaii?
   - ○ visited Alaska or Hawaii?
8. Candice she be over their
   - ○ is over there.
   - ● she is over there.
   - ○ be over their.
   - ○ she is over their.

Friday
9. Isn't that howse on high point road
   - ○ house on High Point road.
   - ○ howse on High Point Road?
   - ● house on High Point Road?
   - ○ howse on high point road?
10. What happen on july 4, 1776
   - ○ happen on July 4, 1776?
   - ● happened on July 4, 1776?
   - ○ happened on july 4, 1776?
   - ○ happen on July, 4, 1776.

p. 89 Assessment 14

Monday
1. Juans father be smart and friendly.
   - ● Juan's father be
   - ○ Juan's father is
   - ○ Juan his father is
   - ○ Juan's father are
2. me and tony be on the same team.
   - ○ Tony and I are
   - ● Tony and me are
   - ○ Me and Tony are
   - ○ I and Tony be

Tuesday
3. dr allen gived her some medicine.
   - ○ Dr. Allen gived
   - ○ Dr Allen give
   - ● Dr. allen gave
   - ○ Dr. Allen gave

4. Karen were absent thursday
   - ○ were absent thursday
   - ○ was absent Thursday.
   - ● was absent Thursday.
   - ○ been absent Thursday.

Wednesday
5. your my bestest friend!
   - ● You're my best friend!
   - ○ You're my bestest friend!
   - ○ You my best friend!
   - ○ You my best friend!
6. bills birthday isn't until December.
   - ○ Bill's birthday isnt
   - ○ Bills birthday isn't
   - ● Bill's birthday isn't
   - ○ Bill's birthday aren't

Thursday
7. vicky she hasn't been here long.
   - ● Vicky she hasnt
   - ○ Vicky hasn't
   - ○ Vicky she hasn't
   - ○ Vicky haven't
8. They move on march 8, 2001.
   - ● moved on March 8, 2001.
   - ○ moved on March 8, 2001.
   - ○ move on March 8, 2001.
   - ○ moved on March. 8, 2001.

Friday
9. Ill meet you by that tree at 430.
   - ○ I'll met you by that tree at 4:30.
   - ○ I'll meet you by that tree at 4:30.
   - ● Ill meet you by that tree at 4:30.
   - ○ I'll meet you by that tree at 4:30.
10. me and jan rided bikes yesterday.
   - ○ Me and Jan rided
   - ● Me and Jan rode
   - ○ Jan and I rode
   - ○ Jan and I rided

p. 90 Assessment 15

Monday
1. wear did i put my pencil?
   - ● Wear did I
   - ○ Wear did i
   - ○ Where did I
   - ○ Where I
2. on may 7 2002, we will have a book sale.
   - ○ On May. 7, 2002.
   - ○ On May. 7, 2002.
   - ○ On May 7, 2002,
   - ● On May 7, 2002.

Tuesday
3. It were relly nice to see dr madison.
   - ○ were really nice to see Dr. Madison.
   - ○ was really nice to see Dr. Madison.
   - ● was really nice to see Dr. Madison.
   - ○ was really nice to see Dr. Madison?
4. The first bell it ring at 805
   - ○ rings at 8:05.
   - ○ It ring at 8:05.
   - ● rings at 8:05
   - ○ ringing at 8:05.

Wednesday
5. Jane sayed, that paper is mine."
   - ○ Jane said, "That
   - ○ Jane said, That
   - ● Jane sayed, "That
   - ○ Jane said, "That
6. o int emmy finded my lost cards.
   - ○ aunt Emmy finded
   - ● Aunt Emmy found
   - ○ Aunt Emmy she found
   - ○ aunt Emmy find

Thursday
7. mr larsen didn't see us arrive.
   - ● Mr. Larsen didn't
   - ○ Mr Larsen didn't
   - ○ Mr Larsen didn't
   - ○ Mr. Larsen didnt
8. I met she on sunday, may 6 2001.
   - ○ she on Sunday, May. 6, 2001.
   - ○ her on Sunday, May 6, 2001.
   - ● her on Sunday, May. 6, 2001."
   - ○ her on Sunday, May 6, 2001.

Friday
9. How long be the mississippi river?
   - ○ be the Mississippi River?
   - ○ are the Mississippi River?
   - ● is the Mississippi River?
   - ○ is the mississippi river?
10. garys dog isn't very large.
   - ○ Gary's dog aren't
   - ○ Gary's dog isnt
   - ● Gary's dog isn't
   - ○ Gary's dog isn't

p. 91 Assessment 16

Monday
1. mr stewart he give me a book to read.
   - ○ Mr. Stewart he give
   - ○ Mr. Stewart he gave
   - ○ Mr. Stewart give
   - ● Mr. Stewart gave
2. My book be call The Great Idea.
   - ○ be called
   - ○ are call
   - ● is called
   - ○ it is called

Tuesday
3. She'll be in miami until wendsday
   - ○ In Miami until Wendsday,
   - ● in Miami until Wednesday.
   - ○ in Miami until Wednesday.
   - ○ in Miami until Wednesday.
4. The football game begin at 700
   - ○ it begin at 7:00.
   - ○ beginning at 7:00.
   - ● begins at 7:00.
   - ○ is begin at 7:00.

Wednesday
5. The bus stop at 205 north main street
   - ○ stop at 205 north main street.
   - ○ stopped at 205 North Main Street.
   - ● stopped at 205 North Main Street.
   - ○ stopped at 205 North Main Street.
6. doug and aaron they fix the problem.
   - ○ Doug and Aaron they fix
   - ● Doug and Aaron fixed
   - ○ Doug and Aaron fixed
   - ○ Doug and Aaron fix

Thursday
7. mrs ellis she come to visit today.
   - ○ Mrs. Ellis came
   - ● Mrs. Ellis she come
   - ○ Mrs. Ellis she come
   - ○ Mrs. ellis came
8. mandy ask, Whats in the bag?"
   - ○ Mandy ask, "What's
   - ● Mandy ask, "Whats
   - ○ Mandy asked, "What's
   - ○ Mandy she asked, "What's

Friday
9. Its to late to get started now.
   - ○ It's too late to
   - ● Its too late to
   - ○ It's to late too
   - ○ Its to late too
10. why dont we try again tomorrow?
   - ○ Why don't we try agin
   - ● Why dont we try again
   - ○ Why don't we try again
   - ○ Why doesn't we try again

p. 92 Assessment 17

Monday
1. I cant wait until 315 today!
   - ○ can't wait until 3:15 today!
   - ○ can't wait until 3:15 today!
   - ● cant wait until 3:15 today!
   - ○ can't waiting until 3:15 today!
2. We watch that show ever monday nite!
   - ○ ever Monday night!
   - ● every Monday night!
   - ○ every monday night!
   - ○ every Monday night!

Tuesday
3. Did it rained more in april or may
   - ○ rained more in April or May?
   - ● rain more in April or May?
   - ○ rain more in April or May.
   - ○ "rain more in April or May?"
4. Julie she live on andover avenue
   - ○ she live on Andover Avenue.
   - ○ live on Andover Avenue.
   - ● lives on Andover Avenue.
   - ○ be living on Andover Avenue.

Wednesday
5. Will you call me saturday at 500
   - ○ Saturday at 5:00?
   - ● saterday at 5:00?
   - ○ Saturday at 5:00?
   - ○ Saterday at 5:00.
6. mr and mrs carson likes to travel.
   - ○ Mr. and Mrs. Carson likes
   - ○ Mr. and Mrs. carson like
   - ○ Mr and Mrs Carson like
   - ● Mr. and Mrs. Carson like

Thursday
7. me and amber want a new puppy.
   - ○ Me and Amber want
   - ● I and Amber want
   - ○ Amber and me wants
   - ○ Amber and I want
8. They be moveing to maryland
   - ○ be moving to Maryland.
   - ● are moving to maryland
   - ○ are moving to Maryland.
   - ○ is moving to Maryland.

Friday
9. I dont have no more questions.
   - ○ don't have any more
   - ● don't have no more
   - ○ ain't got no more
   - ○ don't got no more
10. Mom asked, Wheres Kims hat?
   - ○ "Where's Kim's hat?"
   - ● "Where's kim's hat?"
   - ○ "Where's kim's hat?"
   - ○ "Wheres Kims hat?"

p. 93 Assessment 18

Monday
1. Is Mr. Alva's address 41 south jefferson street
   - ○ 41 south jefferson street?
   - ○ 41 south Jefferson street.
   - ● 41 south Jefferson Street
   - ○ 41 South Jefferson Street?
2. I and jill we play ball at recess.
   - ○ Jill and I play
   - ● I and Jill we play
   - ○ Jill and me play
   - ○ Me and Jill play

Tuesday
3. is mr read helping you today?
   - ○ Is Mr Read
   - ● Is Mr. Read?
   - ○ Is Mr. read
   - ○ Is Mr. Read
4. mom said, dont forget your coat."
   - ● Mom said, "Don't
   - ○ Mom said, "Dont
   - ○ mom said, "Don't
   - ○ Mom said, Don't"

Wednesday
5. The movie last from 700 until 830.
   - ○ last from 7:00 until 8:30.
   - ● it lasts from 7:00 until 8:30.
   - ○ lasts from 7:00 until 830.
   - ○ lasts from 7:00 until 8:30.
6. Darren miss the bus last friday.
   - ○ miss the bus last Friday.
   - ● missed the bus last Friday.
   - ○ missed the bus last friday.
   - ○ missed the bus last Friday

Thursday
7. scott ask, wheres my pencil?"
   - ● Scott asked, "Where's
   - ○ Scott asked, "Where
   - ○ Scott he ask, "Where's
   - ○ Scott ask, "Where's
8. He asked, was you home saturday
   - ○ Was you home Saturday?
   - ○ Were you home Saturday?
   - ● "Were you home Saturday?"
   - ○ "Was you home Saturday?"

Friday
9. Do you remember monday, december 25, 2000?
   - ○ monday, december 25, 2000?
   - ● Monday, December 25, 2000?
   - ○ Monday, December 25, 2000?
   - ○ Monday, December 25, 2000.
10. I has a dog name festus
   - ○ I has a dog named Festus.
   - ● I have a dog named Festus.
   - ○ I have a dog named festus.
   - ○ I have a dog name Festus.